P9-AGO-620

BUDDHISM IN CHINESE HISTORY

BUDDHISM

in

CHINESE HISTORY

Arthur F. Wright

STANFORD UNIVERSITY PRESS · STANFORD, CALIFORNIA

The "Selection of Further Readings," pp. 129-38,
was revised by the author for the 1971 printing.

Stanford University Press
Stanford, California

© 1959 by the Board of Trustees of the
Leland Stanford Junior University
Printed in the United States of America
Cloth ISBN 0-8047-0546-1
Paper ISBN 0-8047-0548-8
Original edition 1959
Last figure below indicates year of this printing:
05   04   03   02   01   00   99   98   97   96

for

MARY CLABAUGH WRIGHT

PREFACE

This volume is based on six lectures presented at the University of Chicago under the joint sponsorship of the Department of Anthropology and the Federated Theological Faculty. It was the hope of my sponsors that the lectures might interest a broad segment of the educated public in a subject that is both integral to the history of a great civilization and relevant to the problem of the interrelations of cultures in our time. The lectures are presented here much as they were given and with the same hope and intent. Annotations and technical details have been kept at a minimum, and a list of further readings has been added for the use of those who may care to explore one or another aspect of the subject.

The six essays in this volume are an attempt at reflective interpretation of one of the great themes in the history of civilizations. No one is more aware than their author of the vast unexplored reaches of history and data that make such an interpretation necessarily tentative and imperfect. Yet I believe the scholar should occasionally stand back and contemplate the whole continuum of time and of problems which give meaning to his specialized studies. He should, it seems to me, report the results of his reflections both to his colleagues in the learned world and to the educated public. In this way he may hope to contribute to the cumulative growth of understanding that is the justification of all scholarship.

The present volume is intended as this sort of report—on work done in a relatively neglected field of study, on conclusions reached, on relationships discerned between different orders of facts or events, on problems encountered and unsolved. Such a report has been made possible by the rapid advance of modern scholarship in the fields of Chinese and Buddhist studies; in the last forty years the mythologized accounts that passed for Chinese history have been critically analyzed, and a few periods and problems have slowly come into focus. In the hands of pioneering scholars, the study of Chinese Buddhism has emerged from the limbo of pious exegesis to become an integral part of the study of Chinese civilization in its historic growth. I owe a particular debt to two of these pioneers: Professor Zenryū Tsukamoto of the Institute of Humanistic Sciences, Kyoto, and Professor Paul Demiéville of the Collège de France.

To acknowledge all the indebtedness I feel to those who have supported and stimulated my studies in the field of Chinese Buddhist history would impose on the reader. Let me therefore mention only those who have been directly concerned with this volume. Dean Jerald Brauer of the Federated Theological Faculty at the University of Chicago and the late Robert Redfield, Robert M. Hutchins Distinguished Service Professor of Anthropology at Chicago, provided the stimulus and the occasion for the first presentation of these essays. Professor Max Loehr of the University of Michigan kindly advised on the selection of illustrations. Mr. Jesse G. Bell, Jr., of the Stanford University

Press gave me the benefit of his unusual editorial acumen, and my wife, Mary Clabaugh Wright, served as expert but indulgent critic. Mrs. Mary H. Johnson typed the several drafts with patience and skill, and Mr. and Mrs. Conrad Schirokauer helped in the preparation of the index. I am indebted to Messrs. Allen and Unwin for permission to quote from the works of the master translator, Arthur Waley, and to the editors of the *Journal of Asian Studies* for allowing me to draw freely on my article "Buddhism in Chinese Culture: Phases of Interaction," which appeared in that journal in 1957. The friendly cooperation of museums and their curators is acknowledged in the list of illustrations.

ARTHUR F. WRIGHT

Stanford, California
January 7, 1959

CONTENTS

LIST OF ILLUSTRATIONS

Eight pages of photographs follow p. 98.

1. Śākyamuni Buddha. Bronze, dated A.D. 338. The earliest dated Chinese Buddhist image thus far discovered. It was made under the non-Chinese dynasty of the Later Chao, whose rulers welcomed the Central Asian missionary monk Fo-t'u-teng. The image represents Chinese efforts to adapt Central Asian prototypes, particularly by severe conventionalization of naturalistic features. Reproduced by kind permission of the owner, Mr. Avery Brundage. Photograph courtesy of Mr. Frank Caro.

2. Mi-lo (Maitreya), the future Buddha. Bronze, gilt. The style is close to that of Central Asian images which were themselves adaptations of Gandhāran models, yet the figure is characterized, in Benjamin Rowland's words, by "a feeling of tremendous exaltation communicated, perhaps most of all, by the great spread and sweep of the outflung robe, like wings unfurled." The inscription (which may possibly be a later addition) dates the figure in A.D. 477 and states that it was made for the benefit of the Empress Dowager and of all living beings; the reference is to the powerful Empress Wen-ming, whose regency saw the consolidation of Northern Wei rule over the north. Courtesy of the Metropolitan Museum of Art, Kennedy Fund.

3. The Bodhisattvas Avalokiteśvara and Mahāsthāmaprāpta. Bronze. The figures are part of a shrine to Amitābha—Buddha of the Western Paradise—made at the pious behest of eight

mothers in 593, shortly after the Sui reunification of China. The Chinese sculptor synthesizes a rich variety of Indian motifs, yet as Laurence Sickman remarks, "the modelling is essentially simple and direct in spite of elaboration of design." The expressions capture the gentleness and compassion of the savior Bodhisattvas. Courtesy of the Museum of Fine Arts, Boston.

4. Eleven-headed Kuan-yin (Avalokiteśvara). Bronze. Period of the T'ang. The figure suggests the graceful opulence and the sureness of touch which characterize the best of Buddhist sculpture in this period of the high tide of Buddhism and of imperial power. Courtesy of the Stanford Museum, The Mortimer Leventritt Collection.

5. Ākāśagarbha Bodhisattva. Wood. One of a set of five such figures brought to Japan from the T'ang capital by the monk Eiun, who was in China during the great suppression of Buddhism and returned to Japan in 847. Now in the Kanchi-in of the Tōji, Kyoto. Ludwig Bachhofer attributes the stiff and lifeless qualities of these figures to the rigid iconographic formulas imposed upon artists by the late form of Buddhism known as Tantrism. In this figure, in contrast to the three preceding figures, the Chinese artist has failed to digest alien elements and achieve his own unity of form. Photograph courtesy of Professor Zenryū Tsukamoto, The Institute of Humanistic Sciences, Kyoto.

6. Lohan in attitude of meditation. Dry lacquer. Dated 1099. Representation of the Lohan—a broad and flexible class of divinities to which the Chinese added at will—conferred great freedom on the artist. It seems likely that the artist Liu Yün (who made this figure for a donor called Ch'iang Sheng and for the spiritual felicity of Ch'iang's children) used as his model a contemporary monk, perhaps of the Ch'an school. Courtesy of the Honolulu Academy of Arts.

BUDDHISM IN CHINESE HISTORY

CHAPTER ONE

THE THOUGHT AND SOCIETY
OF HAN CHINA

One of the great themes in the history of Eastern Asia is the transformation of Chinese culture by Buddhism. We can trace this process across nearly two millennia of time, and we can see it at work in any aspect of Chinese life and thought to which we may choose to direct our attention. What may we expect to learn from an examination of such a process? On the most general level, a better understanding of some of the patterns of interaction between civilizations—patterns with a particular relevance to the cultural problems of our twentieth-century world. Further, we may learn something of the role of religion as a carrier of elements of one great civilization into another. We may be led to critical reflection upon Toynbee's thesis that religion plays a vital role in preserving elements of continuity between a disintegrating civilization and its successor, and that Mahayana Buddhism—as a "church of the internal proletariat" —played such a role during the break-up of Han civilization. And, in turn, we may come to some provisional judgments on the nature of Buddhism as a world religion, on the ways in which it is similar to or different from the other great faiths. As we contemplate the role of Buddhism in Chinese history, we shall become conscious of the great contrasts between Indian and Chinese civilization and be made wary of interpretations that posit "the unity of Oriental culture." Lastly, we shall find clues to an understanding of Chinese civilization: insight into its characteristic and enduring modes of thought; keys to the understanding of its literary and artistic traditions, of its institutions and patterns of individual and group behavior. And, hopefully, we may be led to view these things not as static entities but as aspects of culture changing through time in response to the perennial challenges of changing conditions.

One might choose to survey this vast range of problems and processes synchronically, with separate chapters on the different aspects of Chinese culture which Buddhism affected or transformed, or diachronically, cutting across time barriers. I have chosen the diachronic approach; as a historian, I am accustomed to think of changes in time of a whole civilization, and of the interrelations of all its facets at any moment in time. I particularly wish to emphasize development in Chinese civilization to counteract the Europocentric obsession, persisting from Herder, Hegel, and Marx to Northrop and Wittfogel, that the Chinese—and other "Oriental" peoples—are, in Ranke's memorable phrase of dismissal, *den Völkern des ewigen Stillstandes*.

Such an inquiry into Buddhism and Chinese civilization has its difficulties. Many of these arise from the nature of Chinese Buddhist sources; in volume the Chinese canon alone is approximately seventy-four times the length of the Bible, and problems of organization, textual analysis, and interpretation are formidable. The monographic studies, concordances, and dictionaries which have appeared over the last fifty years are only the first steps toward the analysis of this gigantic corpus of material. When we seek to relate Buddhism to the historic development of Chinese civilization, the problems are multiplied. Here too we are in the early stages of organizing and analyzing the most voluminous record which any people possesses of its own past—a record whose richness and variety reduces the historian almost to despair.[1] Modern historical studies of China have progressed in the last four decades, but they amount to little more than a tentative reconnaissance over a largely uncharted field.

Other problems arise in understanding and interpreting what we do know. When we say that Buddhism affected all aspects of Chinese life and thought, does that mean that it affected them all equally, or in the same way, or to the same degree? Clearly it does not, for we know that the artistic, literary, philosophical and other traditions of a civilization tend to have their separate patterns and dynamics of growth; but when we have recognized this fact we find ourselves knowing little of these distinct patterns, and still less of the way one affects another through time. Again, we know that China, in the long reach of time we shall consider, was composed of many and varied subcultures, but we know little in detail of the characteristic sub-

---

[1] It would require an estimated 45 million English words to translate the twenty-five dynastic histories, and these are only a tiny fraction of the total documentation. The estimate is from Homer H. Dubs, "The Reliability of Chinese Histories," *Far Eastern Quarterly*, VI (1946), 23–43.

cultures of various regions of China and of the ways in
which they affected and interpenetrated one another in
different periods of history.

Happily we now have an increasing variety of monographic studies and of hypotheses that help us to order this
formidable complex of data and problems. Among the
concepts that we shall find useful in the present study is
Robert Redfield's theory of the ways in which elites and
peasantries interact in such two-class peasant-based societies as China's. He refers to the cultures of these two
social strata as the great tradition and the little traditions.
The former is literate, rationalizing, and self-conscious;
it comprises the successive formulations—in art, philosophy, and institutions—of the society's explicit ideals.
The latter are the unselfconscious, uncritical folk traditions
of the peasant villages—the norms of behavior and belief
that are passed down from generation to generation. If
we keep this distinction in mind and watch for the ways in
which the two traditions affect each other—through government, economic arrangements, religion and the arts—
we shall be better able to understand the interaction of
Buddhism and Chinese culture through its successive
phases.

When we speak of phases, we encounter a problem
which has beset historians since the moment when past
time came to be conceived, not as separate mountain peaks
of heroic achievement, but as a process; this is the problem of periodization. The periods into which I divide the
process under study should be taken as hypotheses, as convenient but tentative means of dealing with a vast sweep

of time and a multiplicity of events. These periods are given names which suggest successive modes of interaction between Buddhism and the culture it was invading. But this represents a judgment as to the mode of interaction which was dominant for a certain period of time; it does not mean that any one mode exclusively prevailed. Rather, many of these modes of interaction were present in several of the periods we shall consider, and what may have been a dominant mode in one age was prefigured in the preceding age and echoed in the age that followed.

Before considering the long process which in so many ways transformed Chinese civilization we should consider briefly the society and culture of Han China (206 B.C.– A.D. 220), establishing, as it were, the base points from which change can be measured and understood.

The empire of Han, heir to the forcible unification of China by the Ch'in, was centered in the North China Plain, the land in which a recognizable Chinese civilization had had its beginnings at least a millennium and a half earlier. South China—the Yangtse Valley and below —was a largely uncultivated wilderness inhabited by aborigines; in the far south the Han garrisons controlled northern Indo-China; Chinese colonization of the south as a whole was just beginning. To the west and northwest of the Han empire lay steppe and desert areas, in which the Chinese sought to control the approaches to the empire by war and diplomacy. To the north the empire was protected by the Great Wall, marking the limits of Chinese agriculture; beyond was the steppe land which fostered another and hostile way of life. Far to the northeast the Han had established a flourishing colony near the modern Pyongyang in North Korea, and it maintained control of the lands of southern Manchuria which lay between that colony and the seaward end of the Great Wall.

The social order of the Han empire was basically a two-class system. The ruin of the old feudal aristocracy had been accomplished partly in the sweeping liquidation of feudal institutions by the unifying empire of Ch'in (221–207 B.C.) and finally by the failure of the aristocrats in the civil war which ended the Ch'in regime. The Han ruling house—of plebeian origin—rewarded its loyal relatives and ministers with titles and estates, but these were given and revoked at the emperor's pleasure. A class of people who had served as functionaries of the feudal states and built up family landholdings in the latter part of the Chou period, or under the new empire acquired land through purchase or the opening up of new fields, emerged as the Han elite. They had the wealth and the leisure for learning. They offered their knowledge and skill to the first Han emperor, and thereafter worked to consolidate their position as architects and functionaries of a bureaucratic state, bearers and interpreters of the cultural heritage, guardians of the new social order at both the national and the local level. Below them were the peasants, living in villages, working owned or share-crop holdings, paying the rents and taxes, giving forced labor to military and public works projects decreed from above, existing at the margin of subsistence.

The Han period was an era of rapid economic development. New lands were continually opened up and population grew to perhaps 56 million.[2] Internal trade flourished, and there were great advances in technology and the arts. Fortunes were made and lost in trade and speculation, in mining, iron works, and the manufacture of salt; the gentry-functionaries fought incessantly to control the *nouveaux riches* who often allied themselves with imperial power. The life of the more fortunate upper-class families became increasingly luxurious. They built elaborate houses on their estates, in the towns, or in the capital and furnished them with luxuries from far and near; their women were handsomely dressed and indulged themselves in the latest modes. Han China was expansive, full of bustling life, extroverted. Alexander Soper suggests the spirit of Han life:

> Han was a time of empire-building, of immense new wealth and power, of enlarged political and economic responsibilities. The realistic mood of the age gave small encouragement to anti-social dreaming. . . . For the articulate man of Han—courtier, soldier, or official, city-dweller absorbed in the brilliant pageant of metropolitan life in a busy and successful empire—the most insistent stimulus to the imagination came from the palace, the prime symbol of human greatness, erected now on an unimaginable scale of splendor, vastness, and multiplicity.[3]

This sensuous satisfaction in the new prosperity of China was not limited to those who contemplated the splendors

[2] The figure is for A.D. 156. Cf. Hans Bielenstein, "The Census of China," *Bulletin of the Museum of Far Eastern Antiquities*, XIX (1947), 126, 139–45.

[3] Alexander Soper, "Early Chinese Landscape Painting," *The Art Bulletin*, XXIII (1941), 143–44.

of the capital. Here is an official speaking of life on his estate, to which he retired after being dismissed from office in 56 B.C.:

> When the proprietor has finished his labor and when the season is late summer or the holidays of year's end, he cooks a sheep, he roasts a lamb, he draws a measure of wine, and thus rests from his work. I am from Ch'in and know how to make the music of Ch'in; my wife is from Chao and plays the lute very well. Many of our slaves sing. When after drinking the wine I am warm to the ears I raise my head toward heaven, beat the measure on a jug, and cry "Wu wu." I swing my robe and enjoy myself; pulling back my sleeves . . . I begin to dance.[4]

If such were the preoccupations and pleasures of Han officialdom and gentry, it is scarcely surprising that the thought of the Han has been characterized as a sort of imperial pragmatism in the Roman manner.[5] The synthesis of ideas and values developed in this robust society is a key to much of the later history of Chinese thought. And it is this synthesis, with its accompanying world view, which Buddhism encountered in the first phase of its invasion of China. The conditions under which the Han synthesis took shape and gained authority over the minds of the elite suggest that it was admirably suited to a period of consolidation and expansion of imperial power but that it would prove inadequate for a period of breakdown and crisis.

---

[4] *History of the Former Han Dynasty*, ch. 66. Translated by Henri Maspero in his "Histoire des régimes fonciers," *Etudes historiques* (Paris, 1950), p. 158.

[5] Paul Demiéville, "La Pénétration du Bouddhisme dans la tradition philosophique chinoise," *Cahiers d'histoire mondiale*, III (1956), 20.

The system of ideas which we call Han Confucianism may be viewed as the intellectual response of the new gentry-elite to the problem of rationalizing the new imperial order and their own place in it. Many elements in the new order—hereditary monarchy, for example—were not contrived by the new elite but grew out of historical developments beyond their control. Now they had to be rationalized; and the new order was of such growing complexity that the simple dicta of Confucius, uttered in an earlier period, were clearly inapplicable or inadequate. This suggests why the formulators of Han Confucianism drew so extensively on non-Confucian traditions to develop the structure of ideas which the times and the demands of their own intellects required. I do not believe that Han Confucianism can be wholly reduced to an "ideology" in the sense of a rationalization of a system of power. It is this, but it is also a serious and concerted effort to understand and to order men's knowledge of the cosmos, of human behavior, of culture, and of the cultural past which was their history.

The cosmos, as seen by the Han Confucians, was an all-encompassing system of relationships in which man, human institutions, events, and natural phenomena all interacted in an orderly, predictable way. In developing a rationale of these relationships, the formulators relied extensively on analogies; that is, certain hierachies in nature were taken to be the models for certain human relationships and institutional arrangements. Let us turn to some of the cosmological notions which were part of this system.

Heaven, earth, and man were viewed as an indissoluble

trinity. Tung Chung-shu, the principal architect of the Han system, put it this way: "Heaven, earth, and man are the root of all things. Heaven begets them, earth nourishes them, and man completes them. . . . These three complement each other as arms and legs go together to make a complete body; no one of them can be dispensed with."[6] It followed from this that natural and human events were intimately interrelated and that rulers of men had a cosmic as well as a human responsibility.

Heaven was viewed as presiding over or directing *yang* and *yin*, two complementary modes of being which characterize and animate all phenomena. This concept may have been derived long before, as Granet suggested, from the alternating seasons of primitive agricultural life. It had been further developed by philosophers of several schools, and it was now appropriated by Han Confucianism to explain and interpret both natural and human events. Thus *yang* was seen as the mode of being which included the male, the bright, the creative, the sun, the east, while *yin* included the complementary—not opposite—phenomena: the female, the dark, the recessive, the moon, the west. With the help of this notion, plus a concept of five elements which was also drawn from outside the Confucian tradition, the men of Han worked at classifying all phenomena in an ordered hierarchy whose mutations were accounted for by the complementary oscillation of *yang* and *yin* and by the regular succession of the five elements.

---

[6] *Ch'un-ch'iu fan-lu,* ch. 19, as translated in the draft section on Ch'in and Han thought from the forthcoming Columbia University volume *Sources of the Chinese Tradition,* edited by William Theodore de Bary, p. 7.

The three spheres of heaven, earth, and man, all capable of being analyzed with the aid of these principles of classification and operation, are linked together by the monarch, who is symbolized by the vertical line joining the three horizontal lines in the character *wang*, "Prince." As Son of Heaven the ruler was concerned with the timely performance of ritual, with astronomy and the calendar, with responding to phenomena which could be interpreted as reflecting Heaven's approval or disapproval. In relation to Earth, the ruler was to ensure its harmonious productivity by seeing that proper arrangements were made for agriculture; one way of doing this was by promulgating an agricultural calendar based on observations of the heavenly sphere. Another way was by establishing well-balanced programs for land use and taxation, for trade in the fruits of the earth's bounty. And in doing this he moved into the sphere of Man. There he must first see that his subjects have an adequate means of livelihood, for man cannot perfect himself in virtue until his material needs are met. Once this is done, the ruler is to educate and civilize his people, by teaching the proprieties (*li*), music, and the moral norms. Since men are unequally endowed, only a few can carry this process through to perfection in sagehood. The ruler's obligation to man includes fostering the moral and intellectual fulfillment of the few and using these perfected men in the service of the state; through them society as a whole would be perfected.

If this was to be man's view of himself and the world around him, what was the authority that sanctioned such ideas and provided the keys for their application? Tung

Chung-shu's answer is that these are to be found in the Classics, the distillations of the wisdom of the past:

> The Prince knows that he who is in power cannot by evil methods make men submit to him. Therefore he chooses the Six Disciplines through which to develop the people. . . . These six teachings are all great, and at the same time each has that in which it stands pre-eminent. The *Book of Poetry* describes the human will, and therefore is pre-eminent for its unspoiled naturalness. The *Book of Rites* regulates distinctions, and therefore is pre-eminent for order and refinement. The *Music* intones virtue, and therefore is pre-eminent in its influencing power. The *History* records achievements and therefore is outstanding concerning events. *The Book of Changes* takes Heaven and Earth as its bases, and therefore is best for calculating probabilities. The *Spring and Autumn Annals* rectifies right and wrong, and therefore stands pre-eminent in ruling men.[7]

Note that in commending these six Classics, Tung presents them as preferable to evil methods which the Prince might be tempted to employ—for example, the use of uncultivated officials, the use of military force, or the issuance of uniform and draconian laws, any of which would threaten the still tenuous authority of the new gentry-elite. But, if the Prince, like the Han emperors, chose to make the principles expressed in the Classics the basis of state ideology and education, how was he to make certain that these principles were to prevail over rival doctrines and be correctly interpreted and applied? Tung Chung-shu again provided the answer: Let the ruler suppress deviant doc-

---

[7] *Ibid.*, ch. I, as translated in de Bary draft, p. 12.

trines and let him establish a state-supported center for the
teaching of the orthodoxy by qualified Confucian masters;
further, make knowledge of the orthodoxy, thus acquired,
the basis for appointment to office in the bureaucracy,
whence indoctrinated men could spread the approved teachings through society at large. These principles were gradually given institutional form in the Han Dynasty; and by
the Later Han, the number of students enrolled in the
State University had grown to over 30,000. It was from
this group that officials were appointed. The Confucians,
surviving innumerable checks and challenges, had won predominance for themselves and their doctrines in the Han
world. Before considering some of the effects of these doctrines, we might speculate for a moment on how and why
they won out.

First of all, the Confucianism of the Han had enriched
itself from the teachings of many schools. It had drawn
on Taoism to rationalize man-in-nature; it had incorporated
Hsün-tzu's view of the evil in human nature, thus sanction-
ing at least minimal legal restraints, without which no Chinese emperor would attempt to govern; it had created from
a variety of sources a new rationale of imperial power. It
had thus adapted itself to the realities of the Han empire.
Underlying these accommodations were the common interests of the gentry Confucians and the imperial house.
Both were strongly opposed to the resurgence of feudalism,
which would deprive both the gentry and the monarch of
their hard-won prerogatives. Monarch and Confucians both
required a rationalization of the new state and society in
doctrines which would assure stability. The Confucians de-

veloped these, and the monarch institutionalized them by fiat. The gentry required an order which would guarantee them possession of land and access to power; the emperors needed functionaries, land managers, and tax collectors. The Han Confucians developed principles of political economy —including the primacy of agriculture—which rationalized these relations, and the monarchy gave them institutional force.

The system we have sketched, supported by this range of mutual interests, had far-reaching effects in forming and limiting Han thought. We can only suggest some of these in the compass of this chapter. Analogical reasoning, the forcing of equivalences, was pushed to extremes. The succession of past dynasties had to be worked out to demonstrate the unvarying sequence of the five elements. The state ministries were ranked and subordinated one to another by associating each with an element.[8] The ritual prescriptions were reworked to relate their seasons and performances to the cosmic order. The place of the emperor in the cosmos was elaborated in the specifications of a cosmic house (*ming-t'ang*) in which all the principles of hierarchic order were symbolically expressed.

Confucius, the modest teacher of the state of Lu, was dehumanized and transformed into the prophet and patron saint of a united empire of which he had never dreamed. The old books were pushed, forced, interpolated, and "interpreted" to give them a consistency which their differing ages and authorships belied. The *Book of Changes*, basically a primitive text for taking oracles, was associated with

---

[8] *Ch'un-ch'iu fan-lu*, ch. 59, as translated in de Bary draft, pp. 34–37.

Confucius and made the authority for all manner of analogical constructs. The *Book of Poetry*, in which the people
of an earlier day had sung of their hopes and fears, was
tortured to provide authority for approved moral principles.[9] New "classics" such as the Classic of Filial Submission (*Hsiao-ching*) went far to transform Confucius into
what Granet called the patron saint of a conformist morality.

Imperial Confucianism, which seemed to serve so well
the needs of the monarchy and the elite, had several weak-
nesses which ultimately proved fatal. It had pushed its
analogical reasoning so far that it drew the criticism of
skeptics and naturalists and thus brought the whole highly
articulated structure into doubt. The attacks of Wang
Ch'ung (A.D. 27–ca. 97) began this process of erosion. Han
Confucianism, in its concern with stability and hierarchy,
tended to ossify in a scholasticism devoted to quarrels and
quibbles over the interpretation of authoritative texts; this
weakened its capacity for self-renewal and its ability to
deal with new problems—intellectual or practical—which
arose from changing social and political conditions. Again,
this system of thought had become so completely interwoven with the Han institutional order that when that
order began to break up, Confucianism was weakened;
when the Han fell, Confucianism was utterly discredited.

Social and political changes in the second century A.D.
produced widening fissures in the structure of Han society
and thought. We shall trace the effect of these in our next

---

[9] Cf. J. R. Hightower, *Han-shih wai-chuan: Han Ying's Illustrations of the
Didactic Application of the "Classic of Songs"* (Cambridge, Mass., 1952).

chapter, but it may be helpful to sketch them briefly here. One change of far-reaching importance was the weakening of the Han imperial line. Han Confucianism had made the emperor a cosmic pivot, but in the Later Han he often became in fact the puppet of rival factions, a pitiful pawn in a rapacious struggle for power. These rulers were the victims of a changed socio-political order whose forces their predecessors had struggled to control. Some of the old, established gentry families with a continuous hold on power had become politically entrenched, and their landed wealth had steadily grown until they controlled vast areas and thousands of tenants and slaves. Families which amassed fortunes in trade bought rights to office and acquired larger and larger landed estates. Other powerful families were founded by relatives of eunuchs or of imperial consorts who used their proximity to the throne for ruthless aggrandizement. Great families, old and new, fastened an ever-tighter hold on power. They tended to monopolize office, to manipulate the official selection system in their own and their followers' interests. Their great estates were economically self-sufficient, centers of commerce and manufacturing as well as of farming; they commanded hordes of dependents who did their farm work, kept their sumptuous houses, and could be armed for defense or to carry on their masters' vendettas. The empire was, in effect, being pulled apart by competing centers of power which operated in increasing defiance of any orders from the capital which might threaten them.

In this process the freeholding peasant, whose life was

at best one of grinding toil, found himself in dire straits. As the great estates grew, the tax burden upon him became intolerable, and he had few alternatives before him. Many peasants chose to become the dependents of powerful landlords and work as laborers or sharecroppers on large estates. Other peasants took to banditry, but this was a precarious life. Vast numbers, displaced from the villages by taxation, famine, or flood, lived on relief—a potential recruiting field for dissident uprisings. One estimate is that in the Loyang area in the period A.D. 107–26 there were a hundred times as many displaced persons on relief as there were farmers.[10] The peasant, theoretically the mainstay of the economy and the object of the paternal solicitude of morally cultivated officials, became in fact an object of contempt. The following passage is a poignant evocation of the peasant's plight:

> The gambler came upon a farmer clearing away weeds. He had a straw hat on his head and a hoe in his hand. His face was black, his hands and feet were covered with calluses, his skin was as rough as mulberry bark, and his feet resembled bear's paws. He crouched in the fields, his sweat mixing with the mud. The gambler said to him, "You cultivate the fields in oppressive summer heat. Your back is encrusted with salt, your legs look like burnt stumps, your skin is like leather that cannot be pierced by an awl. You hobble along on misshapen feet and painful legs. Shall I call you a plant or a tree? Yet you can move your body and limbs. Shall I

---

[10] Cf. Lien-sheng Yang, "Great Families of Eastern Han," translated from the Chinese in *Chinese Social History* by John de Francis and E-tu Zen Sun (Washington, D.C., 1956), p. 113.

call you a bird or a beast? Yet you possess a human face. What a fate to be born with such base qualities!"[11]

As the crisis of the peasant economy deepened and signs of social and political malaise appeared for all to see, three kinds of reactions occurred: an intensified power struggle around the throne, intellectual efforts to diagnose and prescribe for the ills of the times, and mass alienation and revolt among the peasantry. These three sets of reactions worked themselves out in the last desperate years of the Han and under its feeble successor states. In doing so they left a society shaken and riven to its foundations—a promising seed-bed for the implantation of alien ideas and institutions.

---

[11] Quoted and translated, *ibid.*, p. 112, from an essay by Ts'ui Yin written in the period A.D. 89–106. For the text, cf. *Ch'uan Shang-ku san-tai . . . wen* (reprint of 1894), ch. 44, p. 5.

CHAPTER TWO

THE PERIOD OF PREPARATION

A poet-official, writing about A.D. 130, evokes for us a scene of imperial revelry in the old Han capital of Ch'ang-an. After describing the course of a gay entertainment, he speaks of the dancing girls:

> Kicking off their vermilion slippers among the trays and flagons, they flapped their long flowing sleeves. Their handsome faces, their sumptuous clothes, were radiant with beauty. With their lovely eyes they cast bewitching glances upon the company. One look at them would make one surrender a city. Even if one were as sternly upright as old Liu Hsia-hui or a Buddhist Śramana, one could not but be captivated.[1]

In these lines we have evidence that Buddhist monks were an accepted part of the life of Ch'ang-an, well enough

---

[1] *Hsi-ching fu* ("Rhyme-prose on the Western Capital"), by Chang Heng (78–139), *Wen-hsüan*, ch. 2, pp. 59–60. Professor Wada Sei believes this to be the first casual reference to Buddhism in China and thus the earliest incontrovertible evidence of its presence there. Cf. Wada's article "Concerning the Date of the Eastward Transmission of Buddhism," in *Sasaki kyōju koki kinen shukuga rombun bunshū* ("A Collection of Essays in Honor of Professor Sasaki's Seventieth Birthday") (Tokyo, 1955), pp. 491–501. But the Buddhist observances of Ying, Prince of Ch'u, in the year A.D. 65, are established beyond reasonable doubt. Cf., *inter alia*, H. Maspero, "Le Songe et l'ambassade de l'empereur Ming," *Bulletin de l'École Française d'Extrême-Orient*, X (1910), 95–130.

known for their ascetic lives to figure in a poet's imagery. There is other evidence that Buddhism had, by this time, been making its way slowly into China for more than half a century. Yet there are, in these early years, few signs of its influence on Chinese life and thought. When we seek an explanation for this, we find that on two quite different levels the preconditions for the spread of its influence had not yet developed. On one level the breakdown of the Han synthesis of thought and institutions had not yet so alienated Chinese of all classes as to make them responsive to new ideas and institutions, particularly those of alien origin. On another level Buddhism had not yet gone through the preliminary process of adaptation which would make it accessible and intelligible to the Chinese. These two processes are the subjects of this chapter, and as we follow them down to the end of the third century, we shall discover some of the grounds on which it seems appropriate to call this period the Period of Preparation.

In resuming our account of the decline and collapse of the Han synthesis, we shall deal first with the deepening crisis as it affected the life and thought of the elite and then turn to the effects of breakdown on the peasant masses.

The many-sided struggle for power around the decaying Han throne became more and more intense in the second half of the second century.[2] Entrenched families of great wealth and an assured hold on lucrative offices watched with alarm the rise of new families whose rapacity

---

[2] In what follows I draw heavily on Etienne Balazs' brilliant article "La Crise sociale et la philosophie politique à la fin des Han," *T'oung-pao*, XXIX (1949), 83–131.

was unchecked by any commitment to the welfare of the realm. Many of these families established themselves through the favor of a member who became empress, and they manipulated the imperial succession for their own selfish ends. The eunuchs, personal servitors of the ruler, used their position of proximity to power to enrich themselves and to secure favors, not only for their relatives but also, as Balazs suggests, for a considerable clientele of merchants and manufacturers. The eunuchs and their group matched in avarice the clans of the empresses' relatives.

Against these powerful groups were ranged the literate provincial gentry who had claimed and rationalized their access to public office in the early days of the Han. As they were successively deprived of power by the contending groups at the capital, they sought collectively to check and repair the decline in their fortunes. As they agitated ceaselessly for reform, their denunciations of their rivals, their prophecies of doom, their outcries against an extravagant and iniquitous government, echoed in the capital and in the provinces. Throughout the country their criticisms of corrupt officials cast in the form of character estimates (*ch'ing-i*) helped to rally the disaffected to the literati cause.

The struggle among the four groups—the entrenched great families, the eunuchs, the *nouveaux riches*, and the intelligentsia—broke into violence in A.D. 166 when the eunuchs moved against the intelligentsia. The sordid sequence of slander, massacre, and assassination which followed weakened the whole upper stratum of Chinese society. Split by conflicting power interests, by violent hatreds and vendettas, by the constant struggle for wealth and property, the upper class oppressed and abused the peasant masses without check or restraint. As the countryside sank further into chaos, the peasantry were without recourse, and waited in sullen discontent for the moment to rise in mass rebellion.

In these years of crisis, reflective Chinese speculated on what had befallen their state and society, on the precarious and unsatisfying lives they led. They sought to diagnose the ills of the time and to find prescriptions. In the early phases of this searching reappraisal of the values and institutions of the Han, they carried further the naturalistic critique of Han Confucianism, but they were reluctant to renounce all the principles of order, hierarchy, and stability which that synthesis had provided. What we then find is a humanizing of Confucianism, a stripping away of the religious and symbolic accretions of the early Han, a search for a new immanent principle of order in the universe, a concentration on the individual human being and the ways in which he might hope to understand and to realize himself. In this quest many thinkers turned to the long-neglected "classics" of Taoism, the *Chuang-tzu* and the *Tao-te ching*, and it was this tradition of Chinese thought—used first to refine and reform Confucianism—that was to become dominant from about the year 250 onward.

But meanwhile scholars were reviving other schools of thought, in an effort to provide an explanation of the ills of the dying Han regime and a formula for the restoration of a workable polity. The School of Alliances (*Realpolitik*) attracted a following among the contenders for power, while others of more speculative temper turned to the long-neglected works of the Logicians for their ideas as well as for their techniques of disputation. The Legalist or Realist tradition commended itself to some who saw harsh and uniform laws as the only means of eliminating abuses and restoring the strength of the state. Wang Fu (ca. 90–165) was led to this view by his searching critique of the society from which he had withdrawn in protest. Ts'ui Shih (ca. 110–?), from his intense practical activity within the decaying political structure, developed a dislike of Confucian homilies equaled only by his hatred of the idle and extravagant holders of capital sinecures. His experience led him to feel that only strong and uniform laws could rebuild state and society, that addiction to ancient formulas would produce nothing but inanition and final disintegration. Such Legalist prescriptions for an ailing society contributed directly and indirectly to discrediting still further the already tarnished Confucian tradition. Yet it was the cataclysm of mass revolt and political collapse which inspired further and more searching attacks on the old orthodoxy, bringing it at last into something like total disrepute.

The peasantry toward the end of the second century was in a mood of desperation. As we noted earlier, the numbers of displaced persons steadily rose, and serious drought and famine brought further suffering and disaffection. The leaders who now appeared offered much to the oppressed and bewildered peasants: religious faith centered on the cults of popular Taoism, the security of a religious community, functions and careers in that community, a reorganized and stable society at the local level. The leaders of religious Taoism set up what we might call sub-governments, regimes which offered the masses those essentials of life which the Han government had long ceased to provide. It was not surprising that the new organizations grew and spread throughout much of the empire. One source says that the leader of the Taoist communities in eastern China commanded the allegiance of the masses in eight provinces which then constituted two-thirds of the empire.[3] As the Taoist leadership consolidated its power, it came to command sufficient resources to challenge the enfeebled Han government. It did so in the Yellow Turban rebellions of 184 in the east and 189 in the west.

For a brief moment the quarreling factions at the Han court united in an organized military effort to crush this threat to their privileged positions. What followed was a holocaust which cost millions of lives and laid waste province after province. The Han forces triumphed, but, instead of uniting in the restoration of orderly government, the warring factions again turned on one another. The literati and the noble families combined to liquidate the eunuchs and their followers, but the structure and authority of government were completely eroded, and power passed to a series of strong men, military adventurers who had built up personal armies and regional bases in the war against the Yellow Turbans. As Balazs says, "With their bands

---

[3] Cf. Howard S. Levy, "Yellow Turban Religion and Rebellion at the End of Han," *Journal of the American Oriental Society*, LXXVI (1956), 214–27.

of tattered and starving mercenaries, vagabonds, ex-con-
victs, landless peasants, nondescript intellectuals without
occupations, men with neither faith nor law, they dominated
the scene for thirty years."[4] One of these military adventurers, Ts'ao Ts'ao, at last managed to gain control of
North China, but his efforts to reconstitute a unified cen-
tralized state were in the end frustrated by the great landed
families which had fastened their hold on local wealth and
power in the declining years of the Han. The Chin dynasty,
which seized power from Ts'ao Ts'ao's heirs in 265, made
its peace with the great families, but in acknowledging the
degree of refeudalization which had occurred, the Chin
fatally compromised its effectiveness as a central government. It was powerless to carry through necessary economic and social reforms. It was soon weakened by a many-
sided struggle for the succession known as the War of the
Eight Princes (290–306), and in much of North China, as
the fourth century opened, the Chin had only a shadow of
effective control over large areas ravaged by famine, plague,
drought, and mass migrations of starving people.

This somber sequence of events had worked the ruin
of a once great empire. Economically, the empire had
fallen far from the height of Han prosperity. Socially, it
was divided, with the great landed families working masses
of sullen serfs in any way they pleased, and with a few
literati families clinging precariously to the shreds of their
traditions in conditions of poverty and insecurity. It was
politically weak and unstable—a prey to internal divisions
and external threats. The breakdown of the ecumenical

---

[4] Balazs, *op. cit.*, p. 91.

order of the Han was virtually complete, and it was this breakdown, as we suggested earlier, which permitted the spread of Buddhism throughout the Chinese world.

Before turning to an account of the ways in which Buddhism was simultaneously being prepared for this expansion, we should consider briefly some of the ways in which thoughtful Chinese continued to analyze their ailing society and to seek solutions to their problems; for it was this urgent quest for a new basis for life and thought that created a favorable climate for the spread of Buddhism among the elite.

Among all the philosophies that were revived in the crisis of the declining Han, it was a form of Taoism that proved to have the strongest appeal in the subsequent period of social and political cataclysm. For a generation thoughtful men only gradually and reluctantly abandoned their efforts to reconcile ideas of order and hierarchy from the Confucian tradition with the ideas they had rediscovered in the classics of philosophic Taoism. But as hope for the restoration of a Han order faded and as Confucian ideas became part of the ideology of the tyrannical but incompetent rulers of a divided China, the interest of intellectuals focused directly on the ideas of philosophic Taoism. They sought in the Taoist classics some clue to their collective plight, some answer to the problems of a civilization in crisis, some formula for the life of a thinking man in a dark and uneasy age. As their search continued, their rejection of earlier Confucian ideals became sharp and complete. Here is a bitter criticism of the old Confucian stereotype of the princely perfected man which stresses his inadaptability in an age of cataclysmic change:

Have you never seen a louse living in a pair of trousers? He flees from a deep seam and hides in a break in the padding, and he regards this as a good home. When he travels he dares not leave the seam; when he moves he dares not come out of the trousers. He feels that he has attained a well-regulated life. When he is hungry he bites a man and regards this as an inexhaustible food supply. But flames over-run the hills, fire spreads, villages and towns are burned up. And all the lice will perish in the trousers, being unable to get out. As for your "princely man" [*chün-tzu*] living in a world of his own, how does he differ from a louse living in a pair of trousers?[5]

The rejection of discredited rules and conventions was complete, but what did these bitter and disillusioned men seek and what did they find in the Taoist tradition? The central idea which they developed and found irresistibly attractive was "naturalness," (*tzu-jan*), which, as Balazs has pointed out, has three associated meanings: (1) nature without human intervention—the self-perpetuating balanced order of nature; (2) the spontaneous liberty of the individual—the endowment, as it were, of the natural man, free of the restraints of convention; (3) the "Absolute"—another name for *Tao*, the principle of harmonious vitality which informs all phenomena.[6]

The men whose thought centered on this principle expressed themselves in a variety of ways. At the most intellectual level they speculated brilliantly about the nature of

---

[5] *Chin-shu* ("History of the Chin Dynasty"), ch. 49, p. 6b. I have modified my earlier translation in the light of Balazs', which appears in his "Entre Révolte nihiliste et évasion mystique: Les Courants intellectuels en Chine au III⁰ siècle de notre ère," *Etudes asiatiques*, II (1948), 40.

[6] Cf. Balazs, "Entre Révolte nihiliste . . . ," pp. 34–35.

life and the social and individual malaise which they found
around them. They did this in the form of dialogues or conversations known as *ch'ing-t'an*, in which the vocabulary
and the metaphors—the range of problems—were defined
by the three books which they found most meaningful:
the *Chuang-tzu*, the *Lao-tzu* (*Tao-te ching*), and the *I-ching*
or Classic of Changes. They also expressed themselves in
behavior, and as one would expect, this often meant the
dramatic flouting of authority, social conventions, and
family morality. They proclaimed the primacy of "naturalness" over man-made rules whose futility was evident in
the corrupt society around them:

> Liu Ling was an inveterate drinker and indulged himself to
> the full. Sometimes he stripped off his clothes and sat in his
> room stark naked. Some men saw him and rebuked him.
> Liu Ling said, "Heaven and earth are my dwelling, and my
> house is my trousers. Why are you all coming into my
> trousers?"[7]

Yet for all their brilliance and courage the neo-Taoists
found no positive means of restoring a viable society. As
time went on, some retreated into pure escapism; others
made a cynical peace with the corrupt tyrants they despised.
And after the great flowering of neo-Taoist thought in the
years 240 to 260, its creative vitality waned and its ideas
became accepted topics of polite conversation in the palaces
of the rich and powerful. Its mode of discourse—*ch'ing-*

---

[7] *Shih-shuo hsin yü*, by Liu I-ch'ing (401–44), ch. IIIA, p. 29. On Liu Ling
and his contemporaries, see Donald Holzman, *La Vie et la pensée de Hi K'ang*
(Leiden, 1957) and "Les Sept Sages de la Forêt des Bambous et la société de leur
temps," *T'oung-pao*, XLIV (1956), 317–46.

t'an—was no longer a speculative instrument but a play-thing of vacuous and cynical aristocrats who watched idly as China slid further into chaos. Arthur Waley has characterized one of these men, the prime minister under whose regime all of North China was finally lost to the barbarians:

> He belonged to one of the most distinguished families in China . . . and was descended from a long line of high officials. He was famous for his great beauty and in particular for the jade-like whiteness of his hands. He subscribed to the theory that though exceptional people acquire transcendent powers through the cult of *le néant* (to use M. Sartre's convenient term) inferior people (among whom he modestly ranked himself) must be content if through their cult of the *néant* they manage (in a dangerous world) to save their own skins. He did his best to take a negative line towards everything, merely to drift with the tide of events.[8]

This suggests the atmosphere among the elite on the eve of the catastrophic loss of North China—a debacle which, as we shall see in the next chapter, had incalculable psychological, social, and cultural consequences in the centuries that followed. Clearly the final breakup of the Han system and the failure to find an acceptable basis for a new order provided conditions in which an alien religion might be expected to find a following.

Throughout this period of the decline and disintegration of the Han order, Buddhism was slowly spreading and taking root in scattered centers throughout the empire. The geographical distribution of these centers testifies to the

---

[8] Arthur Waley, "The Fall of Loyang," *History Today*, No. 4 (1951), p. 8.

fact that Buddhism spread from the Indo-Iranian and Serindian kingdoms of Central Asia along the routes of trade between those kingdoms and China proper; in China itself, the new religion then moved along the main routes of internal trade and communication. And many of the early missionaries had names which clearly indicate that they came from one or another of the great trading centers of Central Asia. The northwestern entrepôt of Tun-huang figures early as a Buddhist center, and there is evidence of early communities in Ch'ang-an and Loyang, in southern Shantung and Anhui, in the lower Yangtse valley, and in the area around the modern Wu-ch'ang. On the far southeast coast Indian traders brought Buddhism to the Chinese outpost of Chiao-chou.

In these early years of its slow penetration, Buddhism did not influence the major social and intellectual movements we have described. There is no evidence that the great thinkers of neo-Taoism knew of it, and the religious Taoism which spread among the disaffected masses was wholly of Chinese origin. Early Chinese princes and emperors who gave Buddhism limited patronage were persuaded for a time that this Buddha might be a divinity of sufficient power to be worth propitiating, and he is often called Huang-lao fou-t'u—a name which suggests that his worshipers saw him as part of the growing pantheon of religious Taoism. The range of the early imperfect translations of Buddhist writings indicates that the few Chinese who became interested in the foreign religion were attracted by its novel formulas for the attainment of supernatural powers, immortality, or salvation and not by its ideas. This early Buddhism was generally regarded as a sect of religious Taoism. And, indeed, as Maspero suggested, Taoist communities may have served to spread certain Buddhist symbols and cults, thus playing a role somewhat analogous to that of the Jewish communities which helped spread early Christianity in the Roman world.

Keeping in mind these rather unpropitious beginnings, we might pause to consider the cultural gulf which had to be bridged before this Indian religion could be made intelligible to the Chinese. No languages are more different than those of China and India. Chinese is uninflected, logographic, and (in its written form) largely monosyllabic; Indian languages are highly inflected, alphabetic, polysyllabic. Chinese has no systematized grammar; Indian languages, particularly Sanskrit, have a formal and highly elaborated grammatical system. When we turn to literary modes, we find that the Chinese preference is for terseness, for metaphors from familiar nature, for the concrete image, whereas Indian literature tends to be discursive, hyperbolic in its metaphors, and full of abstractions. The imaginative range expressed in Chinese literature—even in the Taoist classics—is far more limited, more earthbound, than in the colorful writings of the Indian tradition.

In their attitudes toward the individual the two traditions were poles apart at the beginnings of the invasion of Buddhism. The Chinese had shown little disposition to analyze the personality into its components, while India had a highly developed science of psychological analysis. In concepts of time and space there were also striking differences. The Chinese tended to think of both as finite and to reckon time in life-spans, generations, or political eras; the Indians, on the other hand, conceived of time and space as infinite and tended to think of cosmic eons rather than of units of terrestrial life.

The two traditions diverged most critically in their social and political values. Familism and particularistic ethics continued to be influential among the Chinese even in an age of cataclysmic change, while Mahayana Buddhism taught a universal ethic and a doctrine of salvation outside the family. Whereas Chinese thinkers had long concentrated their efforts on formulas for the good society, Indian and Buddhist thought had laid particular stress upon the pursuit of other-worldly goals.

It was in the third century—when the certainty of the Chinese about their ideas and values was progressively undermined—that these cultural gulfs began to be bridged. It was in that period that there began in earnest the long process of adapting Buddhism to Chinese culture, preparing it for a wider and fuller acceptance among Chinese of all classes.

The first we hear of Buddhist worship combined with a social program for a whole community is the case of a Han local official who, in 191, built a temple in northern Kiangsu and instituted community welfare services designed to ameliorate some of the ills of an impoverished and demoralized peasantry.[9] Significantly, this short-lived

---

[9] See T'ang Yung-t'ung, *Han Wei liang Chin Nan-pei Ch'ao Fo-chiao shih* (*"History of Buddhism in the Han, Western and Eastern Chin, and Nan-pei Ch'ao periods"*) (Ch'ang-sha, 1938), pp. 71–73. Maspero has suggested that this

experiment was carried on in an area which had recently been a center of Yellow Turban dissidence and revolt. It is possible to see in the sketchy record of this community something of the pattern of adaptation to local Chinese society which was to be more fully developed in the following centuries.

Early efforts to translate Buddhist scriptures were carried on under difficult conditions. Patrons of this work were superstitious and fickle; wars and rebellions disrupted many such enterprises. The early missionaries knew little if any Chinese, and their Chinese collaborators knew no Indian or Central Asian language. There was little communication among scattered Buddhist centers, and hence little chance for one translator to profit from the experience of others. These undertakings recall the efforts of the early Christian missionaries in China; both were hopeful poolings of faith, enthusiasm, and ignorance, and the results in both cases were very imperfect translations of alien ideas into Chinese. Little by little the technique of translation improved. But it was not until 286, in Demiéville's view, that a translation appeared which made the speculative ideas of the Mahayana accessible and reasonably intelligible to literate Chinese.[10] This was the work of Dharmakṣa, who had been born in Tun-huang and had spoken Chinese

---

community may have been historically linked to the early Taoistic-Buddhist community at P'eng-ch'eng fostered by Prince Ying of Han, who died in A.D. 71. See "Les Origines de la communauté bouddhiste de Lo-yang," *Journal asiatique*, CCXXV (1934), 91–92.

[10] See Paul Demiéville, "La Pénétration du Bouddhisme dans la tradition philosophique chinoise," *Cahiers d'histoire mondiale*, III (1956), 19–38. This was Dharmakṣa's translation of one of the visions of the *Prajñā-pāramitā sūtra*.

from childhood. Associated with him were a father and a son—two Chinese lay adherents—who were the first serious Chinese Buddhist exegetists. Their efforts were uncertain and fumbling, but they began the long and important Chinese tradition of commentary which interpreted Buddhist ideas in Chinese terms.

In these early efforts—in oral discourse, written translation, and exegesis—to present Buddhist ideas in Chinese language and metaphor, there was necessarily a heavy reliance on the terms and concepts of indigenous traditions. Buddhism had somehow to be "translated" into terms that Chinese could understand. The terms of neo-Taoism were the most appropriate for attempting to render the transcendental notions of Buddhism; also useful were the Confucian classics, which continued to be studied despite the waning authority of the state orthodoxy. Thus, for example, the ancient and honored word *tao*, the key term of philosophic Taoism, was sometimes used to render the Buddhist term *dharma*, "the teaching"; in other cases it was used to translate *bodhi*, "enlightenment," or again *yoga*. The Taoist term for immortals, *chen-jen*, served as a translation of the Buddhist word *Arhat*, "the fully enlightened one." *Wu-wei*, "non-action," was used to render the Buddhist term for ultimate release, *nirvana*. The Confucian expression *hsiao-hsün*, "filial submission and obedience," was used to translate the more general and abstract Sanskrit word *śīla*, "morality."

In the process of translation some passages and expressions deemed offensive to Confucian morality were bowdlerized or omitted. Thus words like "kiss" and "embrace"

—Indian gestures of love and respect for a Bodhisattva—
were simply eliminated. The relatively high position
which Buddhism gave to women and mothers was changed
in these early translations. For example, "Husband supports wife" became "The husband controls his wife," and
"The wife comforts the husband" became "The wife
reveres her husband."[11]

These examples must suffice to suggest the subtle ways
in which Buddhism was prepared and adapted for a Chinese
audience through "translation." A more formal and overt
kind of adaptation is found in the system known as *ko-i*,
"matching concepts." This device, which was prevalent
in the second and third centuries, was probably favored in
the oral exposition of Buddhist teachings. Typically it
consisted of choosing a grouping of Buddhist ideas and
matching them with a plausibly analogous grouping of indigenous ideas. We noted earlier the tendency in Han
Confucianism to analyze phenomena in terms of the five
elements, the five colors, and so on. In *ko-i* the process is
taken up to "explain" Indian ideas, to present the unknown not only in familiar terminology but also in familiar
numerical groupings. For example, the Buddhist Mahā-
bhūtas (four elements) were "paired" for explanatory purposes with the Chinese five elements (*wu-hsing*), and the
five normative virtues of Confucianism (*wu-ch'ang*) were
equated with the five precepts for the behavior of Buddhist

---

[11] Nakamura Hajime, "The Influence of Confucian Ethics on the Chinese
Translations of Buddhist Sutras," *Sino-Indian Studies: Liebenthal Festschrift*
(Santiniketan, 1957), pp. 156–70. The equivalence *śīla–hsiao-hsün* as found in
the *Nāgasena-sūtra* is noted by Demiéville in *T'oung-pao*, XLV (1957), 263.

lay adherents. Many of these pairings were forced. In the words of a Buddhist monk writing in the early fifth century, "At the end of the Han and the beginning of the Wei . . . worthies who sought the essence of Buddhist ideas had, for the first time, fixed lecturing places. They inflated their lectures with *ko-i* and distorted them with paired explanations."[12]

Still another means of adapting and explaining Buddhism to the Chinese was apologetic writing. In such writing generally there was a defense of the alien system which not only extolled its merits but also pointed to ways in which it was either consonant with certain indigenous ideas and values or complementary to them. An apologetic has a special value for the study of the interaction of two traditions because the points at which defense is felt to be necessary are invariably the points of greatest conflict between the two systems of ideas. The earliest apologetic which has come down to us was written at the end of the second century by a Chinese scholar-official who had fled to Chiao-chou (in modern Tongking) to escape the social and political upheavals in his native province. His volume is a kind of cyclopedia of the points at which Buddhism had to be reconciled with or adapted to Chinese tradition. In question-answer form he considers the claims of an alien tradition versus the claims of a native tradition, familism versus monasticism, Sinocentrism versus Indocentrism, the ritual and behavioral pre-

---

[12] Cf. T'ang Yung-t'ung, "On 'Ko-yi,' the Earliest Method by which Indian Buddhism and Chinese Thought were Synthesized," *Radhakrishnan: Comparative Studies in Philosophy Presented in Honor of His Sixtieth Birthday* (New York, 1950), pp. 276–86. My translation from the *Yü-i lun* of Hui-jui (352–436) in *Taishō Daizōkyō*, LV, p. 41b, differs slightly from Professor T'ang's.

scriptions of the Chinese classics versus those of the Buddhist canon, Chinese prudential economics versus Buddhist generosity, and Chinese conceptions of finite human existence versus Buddhist ideas of transmigration. The apologist in his defense of Buddhism is supple and adroit; he reaches into the varied texts of both Confucianism and Taoism to find passages which appear to sanction a Buddhist belief or practice. At last his questioner taxes him:

"You, sir, say that the Buddhist scriptures are like the Yangtze and the Ocean, their style like brocade and embroidery. Why do you not draw on them to answer my questions? Why instead do you quote the *Classic of Poetry* and the *Classic of History*, bringing together things that are different to make them appear the same?"

The apologist replies:

"I knew that you were familiar with the ideas of the Chinese Classics, and for this reason I quoted from them. If I had spoken in the words of the Buddhist scriptures or discoursed on the essence of inaction [philosophic Taoism], it would have been like speaking of the five colors to a blind man or playing the five sounds to one who is deaf."[13]

This process of explaining the unknown in terms of the known was universal in this period of preparation. It would be mistaken to attribute to these scattered apologists, missionaries, and native propagators of the faith anything like a

---

[13] The text of the *Li-huo-lun* here translated is found in *Taishō*, LII, 5. Cf. the translation by Paul Pelliot in "Meou-tseu, ou Les Doutes levés," *T'oungpao*, XIX (1920). The passage also appears in the draft of chap. 15 of *Sources of the Chinese Tradition*.

common strategy, but they all had a common inclination to graft the alien onto native roots. They might well have been following the dictum of the Jesuit Father Bouvet, who wrote some 1,400 years later: "I do not believe that there is anything in the world more proper to dispose the spirit and the heart of the Chinese to embrace our holy religion than to make them see how it is in conformity with their ancient and legitimate philosophy."[14]

As we suggested in our survey of the breakdown of the old order, the ensuing age of questioning, of social and intellectual discontent, rendered Chinese of all classes receptive to a great variety of new ideas and attitudes; to these Buddhism was more readily adapted than it ever could have been to the rigid closed system of the Han.

We may close this chapter with a summary of the progress that Buddhism was making in the increasingly favorable social and intellectual climate of the third and early fourth centuries. The first Chinese Buddhist pilgrim had journeyed to the west and returned with sacred texts. Foreign translators came in increasing number, and Chinese learned to work with them more effectively than ever before. The volume of translated works steadily increased; from an average of only 2.5 works translated per year in the period up to A.D. 220, it rose to 9.4 works per year in the period 265–317.[15] While the range of early translations had been

---

[14] A letter dated August 30, 1697, quoted in Henri Bernard-Maître, *Sagesse chinoise et philosophie chrétienne* (Sien-Sien, 1935), p. 145.

[15] The figures on total number of known works—whether lost or extant— are drawn from Tokiwa Daijō, *Yakugyō sōroku* ("General List of Translated Scriptures") (Tokyo, 1938), pp. 11–17. These numbers are 409 for the period ca. 65–220, 253 for the period 220–265, and 491 for the period 265–317.

narrow and unrepresentative, by the end of the third century a variety of both Hinayana and Mahayana works had been translated. The Prajñā sutras had been introduced, the texts which were later to form the basis of the Pure Land faith had appeared in their first Chinese translations, and basic rules for ordination and the conduct of monastic life were made available for the first time. Buddhist psalmody was introduced, though the story that this was the work of a prince of the Wei ruling house has recently been called into doubt.[16]

Geographically, Buddhism continued to spread, and toward the end of this period it became solidly established in the middle Yangtze valley, as well as in the older centers of the north. By about the year 300, Buddhist establishments in the two northern capitals of Ch'ang-an and Loyang numbered 180 and their clergy some 3,700.[17] There is evidence that Chinese architects had begun to translate the Indian stupa form into the pagodas that were eventually to dot the landscape of the empire, while sculptors and painters had taken the first steps toward the development of a Sino-Buddhist art.

In turning to the next period, we shall emphasize the continuity of this process of cultural interaction. There were no sharp breaks, but rather a slow complex interweaving of Chinese and Indian elements in the steadily changing context of an evolving Chinese society.

---

[16] Cf. K. P. K. Whitaker, "Tsaur Jyr and the Introduction of Fannbay into China," *Bulletin of the School of Oriental and African Studies,* XX (1957), 585–97.

[17] *Pien-cheng lun,* ch. 3, in *Taishō,* LII, 502. The figures are for the Western Chin period, 265–317.

CHAPTER THREE

THE PERIOD OF DOMESTICATION

And, Sir, the last Emperor—so they say—fled from Saragh [Loyang] because of the famine, and his palace and walled city were set on fire. . . . So Saragh is no more, Ngap [the great city of Yeh, further north] no more!

In these words a Sogdian merchant, writing back to his partner in Samarkand, recorded the destruction of the Chinese capital—an imposing city of 600,000—and the shameful flight of the Son of Heaven before the oncoming Huns. The year was 311, and it marks a turning point in Chinese history comparable, as Arthur Waley has suggested, to the sack of Rome by the Goths in 410. Within the next few years, the Chinese had lost their second capital and the whole of North China—the heartland of their culture—to the Huns. The steady erosion of the central power and the refeudalization which was both its cause and its corollary had progressively weakened Chinese control of the northern and central provinces. The effete aristocrats who served the enfeebled throne had neither the will nor the talent to reverse the tide. Wang Yen, the last Prime Minister—he of the jade-white hands and the addiction to the neo-Taoist principle of *le néant*—was taken prisoner and protested to his captors that he had never been interested in politics. The rude chief of the barbarian forces is said to have rebuked him, saying, "You took office when you were quite young, made a name for yourself everywhere within the Four Seas, and now hold the highest office. How can you say that you have never had political ambitions? If any one man is responsible for the ruin of the Empire, it is you."[1]

After the catastrophic loss of the north, members of the Chinese elite fled in large numbers to the area south of the Yangtze, and for nearly three hundred years thereafter the country was politically divided between unstable Chinese dynasties with their capital at Nanking and a succession of non-Chinese states controlling all or part of the north. In the south the Chinese developed a new culture. They clung tenaciously and defensively to every strand of tradition that linked them with the past glory of the Han. Yet they lived and worked in an area that had been a colonial province of the Han—a land whose aboriginal peoples were only gradually converted to Chinese culture. In climate, landscape, crops, diet, and architecture and in many other ways, it contrasted sharply with the northern plains on which their ancestors had begun to shape a distinctive Chinese civilization. Those ancestral plains were now the scene of wars between rival barbarian chiefs, of a succession of institutional experiments designed to perpetuate the rule of alien minorities and

---

[1] The above is drawn from Arthur Waley, "The Fall of Loyang," *History Today*, No. 4 (1951), pp. 7–10. The contemporary Sogdian letter, found in the ruins of a watchtower west of Tun-huang, was translated by W. B. Henning. The account of Wang Yen's interview with the Hun chief Shih Lo is found in *Chin-shu chiao-chu*, ch. 43, p. 25; the rebuke may well have been attributed to Shih Lo by later historians moralizing on the loss of the north.

keep the Chinese in their place. Thus in this period Buddhism had to be adapted not to one but to two evolving cultures, one in the north and one in the south, with different needs. In the following pages we shall examine these two patterns of interaction from the beginning of the age of disunion to the sixth century, when they converged and culminated to usher in the great period of independent growth.

THE SOUTH

When we speak of the area of the Yangtze valley and below in the period of disunion, we must banish from our minds the picture of the densely populated, intensively cultivated South China of recent centuries. When the aristocrats and the remnants of the Chin ruling house fled to the Nanking area early in the fourth century, the south contained perhaps a tenth of the population of China. There were centers of Chinese culture and administration, but around most of these lay vast uncolonized areas into which Chinese settlers were slow to move.

The old provincial families of the Yangtze valley tended to be conservative; they clung to the traditions of Confucian learning which the northern aristocrats had long since discarded in favor of neo-Taoist speculation. Indeed, some southerners blamed the pursuit of "naturalness" among northern statesmen for the catastrophe which had befallen the empire.[2] Tension between the southern Chinese and the

---

[2] See the accusation against the neo-Taoists made by Yü Yü in *Chin-shu chiao-chu*, ch. 82, p. 15. He goes on to say that the barbarian occupation of North China is worse than the decay of the Chou dynasty. On the southern pro-

immigrants from the north arose quickly and persisted for several generations, but in the end both contributed to an elite southern culture. In this culture the literary traditions of the Han were continued and developed; Confucian learning was preserved to provide links with the proud past and an ideology of dynastic and cultural legitimacy which in a measure reassured those who now controlled only the periphery of a once great and united empire. The supremacy of birth over talent, a concept which had gained ground in the last years of the Han, was here affirmed as the social basis of the only remaining "Chinese" state. At the same time the Neo-Taoism brought in by the northern émigrés fitted congenially into the picturesque and dramatic scenery of the Yangtze valley and found devotees among those aristocrats whose shaken confidence was not to be restored by hollow claims that they were the "legitimate" masters of the "Central Kingdom"; these were men who sought something immutable in a time of disaster, or perhaps an escape into nature from a human scene they found intolerable. It was in this cultural milieu that a characteristic southern Buddhism developed in the period of disunion.

This Buddhism was initially molded—in its concepts, its centers of speculative interest, its vocabulary—by neo-Taoism. Much of the discussion of Buddhist ideas was carried on in neo-Taoism's favored mode: the dialogue or colloquy known as *ch'ing-t'an*. As we have seen, the philosophic vitality of neo-Taoism was already a thing of the past,

vincial gentry as preservers of Confucian learning, see T'ang Chang-ju, *Wei Chin Nan-pei Ch'ao shih lun-ts'ung* ("Essays on the History of the Wei, Chin, and Northern and Southern Dynasties") (Peking, 1955), pp. 371–81.

and *ch'ing-t'an* had been transformed from a speculative instrument into the drawing room pastime of an effete and disillusioned aristocracy. But despite its philosophical failures and the political and personal failures of its devotees, neo-Taoism had broken the anachronistic shell of Han Confucianism and widened and deepened the speculative range of Chinese thought. It had gone on to raise questions which could not be answered by reference to the poetical images of its favorite texts, the *Chuang-tzu* and the *Lao-tzu*.

The Chinese converts to Buddhism who began to move among the salons of the southern capital and then to Buddhist centers as these became established throughout the south were men of a certain definable type. Demiéville has suggested that Hui-yüan (334–416) was typical of the Chinese literati who turned to Buddhism.[3] His early training was in Confucian classics, and he taught for a time at a Confucian school. But along with this he developed a strong intellectual interest—or problem interest—in the *Lao-tzu* and the *Chuang-tzu* and achieved a mastery of these texts. Then one day when he heard a famous monk lecture on the Prajñā-pāramitā, Hui-yüan exclaimed that Confucianism, Taoism, and all other schools were but chaff compared with Buddhism. He became a monk, studied, and began to preach. In both his teaching and his writing he relied heavily on Taoist terms and concepts to expound, and thus to modify, the Buddhist ideas that he presented.

Another famous monk who contributed to the spread of Buddhism in the south was Chih-tun (314–66). He

---

[3] Paul Demiéville, "La Pénétration du Bouddhisme dans la tradition philosophique chinoise," *Cahiers d'histoire mondiale*, III (1956), 23–24.

was brilliant, witty, and personable, and a great favorite among the émigré aristocrats at Nanking. He spoke the language of neo-Taoism, and he excelled in the light repartee so esteemed in *ch'ing-t'an* circles. He selected certain ideas from the available Buddhist sutras and related them to the problems of neo-Taoism. Thus, for example, he made a spirited attack on an authoritative commentator who saw in Chuang-tzu's parable of the phoenix and the cicada the meaning that the secret of personal liberty (*hsiao-yao*) lay in conforming to one's lot in the universal order. Chih-tun affirmed that one could and should escape into the infinite like the phoenix and like the Buddhist who frees himself from worldly ties.[4]

Demiéville traces to Chih-tun certain philosophic innovations which were to have far-reaching effects in the subsequent development of Chinese thought. One of these was investing the old Chinese naturalistic notion of *li*, "order," with a new metaphysical meaning drawn from Mahayana philosophy; in this new sense the term came to mean the transcendental absolute principle as opposed to the empirical data of experience, and this form of dualism—new to China —was to appear centuries later as the central conception of a new Confucianism.

Again, one finds in Chih-tun's works, and more fully expressed in the writings of Chu Tao-sheng (365–434), an important polarization which had been prefigured in earlier Chinese thought but only now became explicit. The two poles were gradualism (*chien*) and subitism (*tun*). Chu Tao-sheng and his contemporaries were troubled by the ap-

[4] *Ibid.*, p. 27.

parently conflicting formulas of salvation offered in the Hinayana and Mahayana texts that had by now been translated. The former appeared to prescribe an age-long and arduous accumulation of positive karma leading to ultimate release into nirvana. The Mahayana texts, on the other hand, offered the seeker after salvation the help of Buddhas and Bodhisattvas and the possibility of a single and sudden moment of enlightenment. Chinese Buddhists thus felt that they discerned in Buddhism two paths to truth and liberation. Gradualism (*chien*) was an approach to the ultimate reality (*li*) by analysis, the accumulation of particulars, long study; it also implied a sense of reality which presupposed plurality, a set of spatially and temporally defined aspects of reality to which a succession of graded methods provided the key. Gradualism, though elaborated with a subtlety unknown to pre-Buddhist China, is basically akin to the native Confucian tradition with its prescriptions for the slow accumulation of knowledge and wisdom. Subitism (*tun*), on the other hand, meant the one as opposed to the multiple, totality as opposed to particulars, the complete apprehension of reality in a sudden and complete vision. Subitism, in Demiéville's view, was clearly associated with the indigenous Taoist tradition; at the same time it was a peculiarly Chinese reaction—found among many who studied Buddhism—against the prolixity of Buddhist writings, their attenuated chain reasoning, and their scholastic rigor of demonstration. This polarization was later to be the center of controversy within the school of Ch'an (Zen), and still later characterized the principal division within a revived Confucianism.[5]

---

[5] *Ibid.*, pp. 28–35. Cf. also Walter Liebenthal, "The World Conception of Chu Tao-sheng," *Monumenta Nipponica*, XII (1956), 87–94.

In addition to such developments in the philosophic realm, Buddhist monks in the south introduced certain practical and doctrinal innovations that were in keeping with the intellectual climate of their time. Hui-yüan, by reason of his versatility, exemplifies in his career many of these innovations. He and men like him did not merely cater to the capital aristocrats but built their own centers of devotion and teaching, often in a mountain fastness. They attracted lay patrons, and the number of temples steadily increased. Hui-yüan was the first to teach the attainment of salvation through faith in Amitābha and thus laid the foundations for the great Pure Land sect, which was eventually to become the most popular form of Buddhism in eastern Asia. While his own writings are full of Taoist thought and terminology, he was indefatigable in his search for a sounder and fuller understanding of Indian Buddhist ideas. To this end he sent disciples to Central Asia to bring back texts, and was in touch with at least six foreign translators.[6]

Hui-yüan was also called upon to defend the Buddhist clergy against the threat of government control or suppression. In his defense one can discern many of the points of conflict between Chinese views of life and society and the principles of the imported faith. Hui-yüan was not militant; he sought a *modus vivendi*, and, by dexterous appeals to the Taoist classics, he managed to make a far better case than he would have been able to make if Confucianism had maintained its erstwhile authority. He argued strongly that a subject who becomes a monk cuts his ties with the world of

---

[6] Cf. Leon Hurvitz, " 'Render unto Caesar' in Early Chinese Buddhism," *Sino Indian Studies, Liebenthal Festschrift* (Santineketan, India, 1957), pp. 87–88.

material gain and personal reward; since he does not seek to benefit from the arrangements maintained by secular authority, he should not be obliged to pay homage to the reigning prince. But, he conceded, lay Buddhists do seek worldly goals and owe secular authority full respect:

> Those who revere the Buddhist teaching but remain in their homes are subjects who are obedient to the transforming power of temporal rulers. Their inclination is not to alter prevailing custom, and their conduct accords with secular norms. In them there are the affections of natural kinship and the proprieties of respect for authority. . . . The retribution of evil karma is regarded as punishment; it makes people fearful and thus circumspect. The halls of heaven are regarded as a reward; this makes them think of the pleasures of heaven and act accordingly. . . . Therefore they who rejoice in the way of Sākya invariably first serve their parents and respect their lords. . . .[7]

Buddhism was interpreted by Hui-yüan as acquiescent in the political and social arrangements of a world of illusion: Buddhism ameliorates and assuages but it does not seek reform. Yet Buddhists worked hard and skillfully to win the favor of the southern rulers, offering them not only the hope of personal salvation but new, potent, and colorful rituals invoking the help of Buddhist divinities for the well-being of the realm, for the warding off of evil. The treasure-trove of Buddhist legend also offered a new model for kingly behavior—that of the Indian Cakravartin-rāja, the king who rules well and successfully through devotion to Buddha and

---

[7] *Hung-ming chi* 5, in *Taishō*, LII, 30. My translation differs somewhat from that of Hurvitz, *op. cit.*, p. 98.

his teaching—and the related model of the munificent do-nor, the Mahādānapati, whose gifts to the Buddhist order for the benefit of his fellow creatures make of him some-thing akin to a living Bodhisattva. These models had a strong appeal to monarchs whose life and power were always uncertain, whose claims to "legitimate" descent from the Han were scant reassurance after decades of political in-stability.

Among the monarchs who embraced and promoted Bud-dhism, the best known is Emperor Wu of the Liang (reigned 502–49). He himself took the Buddhist vows and on sev-eral occasions literally "gave himself" to a Buddhist temple, requiring his ministers to "ransom" him with huge gifts to the temple. On the Buddha's birthday in 504 he ordered the imperial relatives, the nobles, and the officials to forsake Taoism and embrace Buddhism. In 517 he decreed the destruction of the temples of the Taoists—whose religion had steadily grown in power and influence (partly through its selective borrowing from Buddhism)—and ordered the Taoist adepts to return to lay life. He patterned himself after the new Buddhist model of kingly behavior, and his efforts won him titles which suggest the fusion of Chinese and Buddhist political sanctions. He was called Huang-ti p'u-sa (Emperor Bodhisattva), Chiu-shih p'u-sa (Savior Bodhisattva), and P'u-sa t'ien-tzu (Bodhisattva Son of Heaven).[8]

Yet neither wealth nor political power in the south was concentrated in the throne. Rather the great territorial fami-

---

[8] On this ruler, see Mori Mikisaburō, *Ryō no Butei* ("Emperor Wu of the Liang") (Kyoto, 1956), especially pp. 134–69.

lies came to control and manipulate the throne, and to monopolize the selection of officials. Among these great families and among the less well-to-do but literate families Buddhism gradually attracted a large following. The metropolitan officials and the leaders of the intellectual and social life of the capital were greatly impressed by Vimalakīrti, central figure in one of the most influential Buddhist scriptures of the time. He was not a naked ascetic but a rich and powerful aristocrat, a brilliant talker, a respected householder and father, a man who denied himself no luxury or pleasure yet possessed so pure and disciplined a personality that he changed all whom he met for the better. Here was a new model for aristocratic lay Buddhists who were attracted by the ideals of Buddhism but had no desire to renounce their worldly pleasures. There was also, for the rich and powerful, new satisfaction in the lavish building of temples and retreats in the developing style of Chinese Buddhist architecture. Here was an opportunity for display, for "conspicuous consumption," which had the added charm of accumulating merit toward future salvation. And, in many cases, the temples built and endowed by the rich served both as their personal retreats and as shrines for the perpetual performance of their family rites.

Others among the literate were deeply moved by the new Buddhist vision of reality and salvation, became the disciples of certain noted monks, and entered the order. Still others took orders simply out of disgust with the corrupt political life which denied them the satisfaction of a public career, or out of disillusionment with the threadbare formulas of neo-Taoism. As Buddhism became more and more generally accepted, the literate monks found in it counterparts of those scholarly and cultural satisfactions which their ancestors had found in Confucianism. Many collected books; some became noted calligraphers or writers in a particular genre. Others became antiquarians or historians of Buddhism or specialists in one or another Buddhist text, just as in an earlier day they might have specialized in one of the Confucian classics. A life of devotions and scholarship in some temple set in the midst of lovely scenery not only offered satisfactions which the troubled world outside could scarcely provide, but was fully sanctioned by the Bodhisattva ideal of renunciation and work for the salvation of all creatures. This conception of the monastic vocation—withdrawal, gentle contemplation, scholarship, and speculation—proved perennially attractive to literate Chinese in the centuries that followed.

Of popular Buddhism in the south we know far less than we know of the Buddhism of the elite. There is evidence of a sharp clash in the countryside—often cast as a contest of charismatic and magical powers—between the Buddhist clergy and the Taoist adepts. The Taoists had established roots in parts of the south from the time of the Yellow Turban uprising, and in these places Buddhism had to struggle to win a mass following. Monks from various temples would spend part of each year working among the populace. Their rituals and charms, their promise of salvation cast in simple terms, perhaps driven home by one of the stories which dramatized the working of karmic law, undoubtedly won them adherents. As often as possible, in both south and north, they deftly introduced Buddhist elements into the old village associations which existed for the support of fertility rites or other observances.[9] Many commoners attached as hereditary serfs to the growing landholdings of the Buddhist temples must have increased the number of Buddhists among the masses. So perhaps did the increasingly large and diversified class of artisans which catered to the needs of the temples and monasteries.

As Chinese colonists slowly moved into the old aboriginal areas, they brought Buddhism with them, often in the person of officials or incoming gentry who combined Buddhism as a personal religion with old Confucian-rooted ideas and techniques for bringing Chinese civilization to "the natives." Buddhism was seen as a "civilizing" competitor against native shamanistic rites—a field of competition in which Confucianism was ill-equipped.[10]

In the south, then, we find Buddhism adjusting to elite and popular culture, interacting with southern philosophical and literary traditions, developing its beliefs and practices in response to a society which was inadequately served by the traditions it had inherited from the dying Han empire. Let us now consider the concurrent progress of Buddhism in North China.

THE NORTH

The area north of the Yangtze which was relinquished to alien rule in 317 was not, we should remind ourselves, the

---

[9] See Jacques Gernet, *Les Aspects économiques du Bouddhisme dans la société chinoise du Ve au Xe siècle* (Saigon, 1956), pp. 245–69. I have reviewed this important study in *Journal of Asian Studies*, XVI (1957), 408–14, under the title "The Economic Role of Buddhism in China."

[10] Cf. Hisayuki Miyakawa, "The Confucianization of South China." To appear in *The Confucian Persuasion* (Stanford, 1959).

North China of today. For Chinese of that time it *was* China, referred to in their writings not only as "the central plain" (*chung-yüan*) but by the historic and value-laden term *chung-kuo*, "the Central Kingdom." It was the scene of the great cultural achievements of the Chinese people, the homeland of their philosophers, the land on which the great empires of Ch'in and Han had first given political unity to the people of China. The loss of this land to despised barbarians reduced the émigré aristocrats of Nanking to tears of remorse and self-pity. Their relatives who remained in the north—and they were an overwhelming majority of the literate class—endured a succession of alien regimes which outdid one another in tyranny, rapacity, and incompetence. Chinese invariably served these regimes, partly out of self-interest—the protection of family property—but partly in the hope that they could meliorate the harshness of the barbarians and work toward the reestablishment of a Confucian polity and society.

The society of North China, in the early years of disunion, was a deeply divided one. The fissures ran in many directions. The alien minorities—generally, at first, horsemen contemptuous of farmers—were shortly divided into two groups: those who favored different degrees of Sinicization and those who clung to the traditions of their steppe ancestors. Often before they had resolved this difference they were overwhelmed by new invaders from beyond the Great Wall. Racial hatred between one non-Chinese group and another was ferocious, and between the Chinese and the alien intruders it often broke into violence and mass slaughter. Endless wars laid waste the land; levy after levy tore the peasant from his fields. The great landed magnate of today would be killed tomorrow, and those who had sought his protection would become the slaves of a stranger. It is against this background of tension and insecurity that Buddhism began to find its way into this society.

The pioneer missionary in the north was a Kuchan, Fo-t'u-teng. He was on his way to the Chin capital of Loyang, probably with the aim of becoming a translator in one of the imperially supported temples there. Instead he arrived just as the great capital was sacked and burned, and he found himself in the camp of a rude, illiterate Hun who was on his way to control of most of North China. The instinct of the true missionary was equal to the occasion. "He knew that Lo (the Hun chieftain) did not understand profound doctrines but would only be able to recognize magical power as evidence of the potency of Buddhism. . . . Thereupon he took his begging bowl, filled it with water, burned incense, and said a spell over it. In a moment there sprang up blue lotus flowers whose brightness and color dazzled the eyes."[11] Lo was deeply impressed, and for the next two decades he was an ardent patron of Buddhism.

Throughout the north the initial foothold was won for Buddhism by the demonstration to credulous barbarians of its superior magical power, the charisma of its monks which helped to win battles, bring rain, relieve sickness, and assuage the spasms of remorse which overcame the simple barbarian chiefs after some particularly ghastly slaughter. With the favor thus won Buddhist monks began to establish

[11] Cf. A. F. Wright, "Fo-t'u-teng: A Biography," *Harvard Journal of Asiatic Studies*, XI (1948) 321–71.

centers, to teach, and to spread their religion throughout the north. In the long run this foreign religion commended itself to alien rulers on a number of grounds besides that of its superior magical power. First of all, it was a religion alien to China. When the barbarian chiefs learned enough to know that their own tribal ways would not long sustain them in control of North China, they were reluctant to adopt the Confucian principles urged on them by wily Chinese advisers; this course might well mean the loss of cultural identity, the cession of a fatal amount of power to the subject Chinese. Buddhism provided an attractive alternative, and its monks—many of them foreigners—seemed, in their total dependence on the ruler's favor and their lack of family networks, to be useful and trustworthy servants. A further point in favor of Buddhism was that its ethic was universalistic, applicable to men of all races, times, and cultures; it thus seemed the very thing to close some of the social fissures that plagued these regimes and to contribute to the building of a unified and pliable body social.

These apparent advantages won for Buddhism the support and protection of a succession of autocratic rulers and, through this support, an unequaled opportunity to spread throughout the whole of society. From the mid-fourth century onward, we find extraordinary expansion at all levels. At the topmost level the rulers and their families became lavish patrons of the Buddhist church, making munificent gifts of treasure and land to the clergy, building sumptuous temples and monasteries, supporting such great works of piety as the cave temples of Yün-kang. In many of the great temples, regular official prayers were said for the welfare of the ruling house and for the peace and prosperity of the realm. Upper-class Chinese followed the pattern of their counterparts in the south: a substratum of solid Confucian training at home, unsatisfying experiments with neo-Taoism, and then conversion to a faith which seemed to explain the ills of a stricken society and to offer hope for the future. It is from this class that the great thinkers and teachers of northern Buddhism in this period were recruited.

The grandees—alien, Chinese, or of mixed stock—took as much delight in lavish building as the southern aristocrats. Some sought to expiate past crimes, others to win spiritual credit, others to impress the populace or their pious overlords. There was a veritable orgy of temple-building, monasteries were heavily endowed, new Buddhist statues and paintings were commissioned, and the sacred texts were copied and recopied with loving care. Many of these buildings and pious works reflected a family interest, and Buddhist monks became the priests of the ancestor cults of their patrons.

Among the masses, both alien and Chinese, Buddhism found a wide following. As in the south, it was often grafted onto existing rural cults. But in the north, at least in the early part of this period, Buddhist monks did not have the competition of an entrenched religious Taoism, and the peasantry were converted *en masse*. The Buddhist clergy not only offered the consolation of a simple faith, but, as favored instruments of government, often brought into the rural areas medicine, relief grain, and other practical benefits which in an earlier day might have been provided by local officials or rural gentry. The great monasteries, as Gernet has shown, became entrepreneurs; at first they were given relatively infertile highlands, often in localities which were economically undeveloped or in decline. Later, however, they expanded and developed their holdings into the lowlands, and, in addition to bringing more land under cultivation, they developed water mills, oil presses, and local manufactures. They increased their wealth by establishing pawnshops, holding auctions, and sponsoring temple fairs. Often they came to control villages or clusters of villages, whose people became hereditary serfs of the temple.

In many respects the Buddhist faith in North China cut across class lines and helped to unite a divided society. The local maigre feast, held on a Buddhist holiday, was an occasion of community fellowship in which social frictions were forgotten. Contemporary inscriptions show that Chinese and alien officials, local notables, the Buddhist clergy, and commoners often collaborated in building temples, making votive images, and other pious works. Moreover, Buddhist inscriptions—from the monumental cave-temples of Yünkang and Lung-men to the crudest images—testify to the fact that Buddhism was everywhere reconciled to and interwoven with the family cult. A typical inscription of the period might read: "We respectfully make and present this holy image in honor of the Buddhas, Bodhisattvas, and pray that all living creatures may attain salvation, and particularly that the souls of our ancestors and relatives [names given] may find repose and release." The favored object of faith and devotion was more and more the Buddha Amitābha, who presided over the Western Paradise.[12]

---

[12] Tsukamoto Zenryū, tables in Mizuno and Nagahiro, *Ryūmon sekkutsu no kenkyū* ("A Study of the Buddhist Cave-Temples at Lung-men") (Tokyo, 1941), following p. 449. Although these tables record only changes in the objects of

The growing strength of the Buddhist faith and its organizations inevitably caused the rulers of North China some misgivings. These misgivings were deepened by widespread abuses of clerical privilege, by mass retreat into holy orders to escape the corvée and taxation, and by the wholesale and often fraudulent transfer of land-titles to the tax-exempt monasteries and temples. There were further grounds for uneasiness in the rise of uneducated and undisciplined village clergy who often in their preaching exploited the apocalyptic vein in Buddhism for subversive purposes.

The two principal opponents of Buddhism were quick to point out these abuses. The clergy of religious Taoism, who invaded the north in the fifth and sixth centuries, hoped thereby to undermine state support of Buddhism and wrest control of the populace from their Buddhist rivals. Chinese officials, striving always to persuade their alien masters to reconstitute a Confucian state in which the educated gentry would have the key role, drew on the arsenal of argument in their own tradition of political economy; they argued with increasing conviction that the Buddhist church was parasitic and subversive, a blight and an anomaly.

The efforts of these two groups, playing upon the fears of the rulers, brought two developments in Buddhist-state relations that are characteristic of the north. One was the setting up of a clerical bureaucracy whose head was responsible to the throne for all matters relating to ordination standards, conduct of the clergy, and the management of Buddhist property. This system of control, modeled on the

---

devotion in the Lung-men caves, there is reason to believe that the trend toward Amitābha worship was general.

Chinese civil bureaucracy and guided by similar rules of procedure and organization, was to persist until recent times. The other principal development was an attempt, made in 446–52 and again in 574–78, to impose drastic restrictions on Buddhist organizations and activities. These two attempts were made in different circumstances, but they have some common features which are worth noting. The considerations which led to both were mainly political and economic; the instigators in both cases were Taoists and Confucians in uneasy alliance against their common rival; the suppressions were both ineffective, and both were followed by the rehabilitation of Buddhism and dramatic expiatory acts on the part of the rulers who succeeded the would-be suppressors. Both illustrated northern Buddhism's heavy dependence on the favor of autocratic rulers, but the aftermaths of both demonstrated that Buddhism had become too much a part of the culture and life of the north to be eliminated by imperial edict.

The northern Buddhist solutions to the problem of the relation between secular and religious powers were notably different from those advocated in the south by Hui-yüan and his successors. The southerners had to reconcile Buddhism with an aristocratic state and society, while the northerners had to deal with an autocracy. In the Northern Wei the simple proposal had been made to regard the reigning emperor as a Buddha incarnate and thus resolve the conflict of loyalties. In arguing for the suppression of Buddhism in 574, one group maintained that it was not the Buddhist religion but the church that was bad, and that if the church were eliminated, the state would become one vast and harmonious temple—(P'ing-yen ta-ssu)—with the ruler presiding over his believing subjects as a Buddha.[13] Northern Buddhism was, in sum, far closer to Caesaro-papism than that of the south, where Buddhists had been content to make of the politically feeble emperors great lay patrons (mahā-dānapati) and wielders of kingly power for the good of the faith in the manner of the Indian Cakravartin-rāja.

The north, in these years, was the major center of translation and of the dedicated pursuit of a deeper understanding of Buddhism. Despite its political instability, the north was more open to foreign missionaries arriving from Central Asia than the relatively isolated south. These great missionaries came in increasing numbers through the fourth and fifth centuries, and more and more learned Chinese joined with them in the immense effort to translate Buddhist ideas into Chinese terms. One of the great Chinese monks was Tao-an (312–85), a disciple of the pioneer missionary monk Fo-t'u-teng. Tao-an worked indefatigably with foreign translators, and it was he who developed a mature theory of translation which recognized the danger that Buddhist ideas might be dissolved beyond recognition into the neo-Taoist concepts first used to translate and interpret them.

The emancipation of Buddhist ideas from Taoism, which was still incomplete at Tao-an's death, was to be furthered by Kumārajīva, the greatest of the missionary translators and perhaps the greatest translator of all time. Kumārajīva arrived at Ch'ang-an in 401 after learning Chinese during a long captivity in northwest China, where the local warlord

---

[13] See A. F. Wright, "Fu I and the Rejection of Buddhism," *Journal of the History of Ideas*, XII (1951), 34–38, for references to Tsukamoto Zenryū's three important studies of the Northern Chou suppression.

had held him for his charismatic power. Fortunately he found a royal patron, and Chinese monks were assembled from far and near to work with him in translating the sacred texts. This was a "highly structured project," suggestive of the cooperative enterprises of scientists today. There were corps of specialists at all levels: those who discussed doctrinal questions with Kumārajīva; those who checked the new translations against the old and imperfect ones; hundreds of editors, subeditors, and copyists. The quality and quantity of the translations produced by these men in the space of eight years is truly astounding. Thanks to their efforts the ideas of Mahayana Buddhism were presented in Chinese with far greater clarity and precision than ever before. Śūnyatā—Nāgārjuna's concept of the void—was disentangled from the Taoist terminology which had obscured and distorted it, and this and other key doctrines of Buddhism were made comprehensible enough to lay the intellectual foundations of the great age of independent Chinese Buddhism that was to follow.

Toward the end of the period of disunion we have been considering, the cultures of north and south were tending to influence each other and thus to reduce the differences which had developed in the course of their separate evolution over nearly three centuries. Buddhist monks from the north migrated to the south, and southern monks went north. The great translations made in the north were soon circulating in the temples of the south. Buddhists of north and south thus developed common philosophical and textual interests, and styles of Buddhist art in north and south began to affect one another.

Socially and politically the north tended, toward the end of this period, to become more and more Sinicized. Rulers of alien stock still occasionally asserted their separateness and insisted on their dominance, but intermarriage had broken down many of the barriers between Chinese and barbarian, and the rehabilitation of China's agricultural system had made the Chinese increasingly indispensable to the alien rulers. Most important of all, many of these rulers dreamed of conquering the south and reuniting China under their sway. To this end they schooled themselves in Chinese history, political ideology, and statecraft, and in so doing they inevitably came to adopt Chinese ideas and attitudes in these spheres. Yet cultural and institutional differences in the late sixth century were still many and great. Buddhism, as we shall see, played an important role in reducing these differences and thus in laying the foundations of the unified, and eventually Confucian, society that was to come.

CHAPTER FOUR

THE PERIOD OF INDEPENDENT GROWTH

When a young official of the non-Chinese state of Chou seized the throne from his lord in 581, he proclaimed the dynasty of Sui. By ruthlessness, tenacity, and good luck he consolidated his hold on North China and began to plan—as so many northern rulers had before him—the conquest of the south and the unification of all China under his sway. His planning was careful; his military, economic, and ideological preparations were thorough. In 589 his forces overwhelmed the last of the "legitimate" dynasties at Nanking, and after nearly three hundred years China was once again politically united.

Yet military and political conquest alone was not sufficient to destroy the effect of centuries of division, of diverging traditions, of varying habits, customs, and tastes. Life in the north tended to be more austere; food, clothing, and manners were simpler; monogamy and the extended family prevailed in contrast to widespread concubinage and the conjugal family in the south. The southerners considered northern literary style crude and cacophonous, "like the braying of donkeys and the barking of dogs." The northerners regarded southern literature as effete, the work of dilettantes, of men who lacked the martial virtues. The Sui rulers, in their dream of recreating from these contrasting societies a stable, harmonious, and unified order on the model of the great Han, availed themselves of the three traditions which, in different ways, commanded the loyalties of elite and peasantry alike.

Their approach to religious Taoism was simple and straightforward. They recognized it, paid honors to Lao-tzu, the apotheosized philosopher who was its principal deity, and placed its organization under state control and regulation.

Of far greater historical significance was the selective revival of Confucianism. Its ritual-symbolic procedures were refurbished for use in the court and countryside to give the Sui an aura of legitimacy and to demonstrate that the Sui was reviving the ecumenical empire of the Han. The civil virtues of Confucianism were proclaimed as norms for all the people, and knowledge of the Confucian classics was decreed as the basis for a revived examination and selection system. Despite its eclipse, the Confucian tradition had a monopoly of certain resources, notably in political theories and in techniques for political and social control, which neither of its rivals had come close to matching. Yet this was a limited revival, for Confucianism as a total intellectual system was by now patently anachronistic. It was not until three hundred years later that men began in earnest the task of making Confucianism once again responsive to the intellectual, spiritual, and social needs of Chinese of all classes.

Buddhism, by the end of the period of disunion, had a wide following among peasantry and elite in north and south alike. It thus commended itself to the reunifying dynasty of

Sui, and to its successor, the great T'ang, as an instrument for knitting together the two cultures. Both dynasties made it a matter of imperial policy to patronize Buddhist establishments and clergy, to sponsor pious works, and to build and support temples in the capital and the provinces. The Sui founder presented himself to the populace as a universal monarch, a pious believer and a munificent patron of the church (mahādānapati). Early in his reign he proclaimed the religious ideology for the military campaigns on which he was about to embark:

> With the armed might of a Cakravartin king, We spread the ideals of the ultimately enlightened one. With a hundred victories in a hundred battles, We promote the practice of the ten Buddhist virtues. Therefore We regard the weapons of war as having become like the offerings of incense and flowers presented to Buddha, and the fields of this world as becoming forever identical with the Buddhaland.[1]

The Sui and T'ang emperors, by innumerable donations and pronouncements, recognized the fact that their subjects were Buddhists and that Buddhism had its uses for assuring social stability, unity, and peace. At the same time, with the history of recent dynasties in mind, they were anxious to guard against the resurgence of a Buddhist church as an *imperium in imperio*. They repeatedly took steps to control its growth and to abort any subversive tendencies among the

---

[1] For a discussion of Buddhism in the Sui, see A. F. Wright, "The Formation of Sui Ideology," in John Fairbank, ed., *Chinese Thought and Institutions* (Chicago, 1957), pp. 93–104. The Edict of 581 is found in *Li-tai san-pao chi*, ch. 12, *Taishō*, XLIX, 107c.

Buddhist communities. State control through a clerical bureaucracy in the Northern Wei manner was instituted, and there were repeated orders for the proper examination and screening of aspirants to the clergy. Monks were required to obtain official ordination certificates, and to have them frequently renewed. Temples were given official charters, and unauthorized temple-building was forbidden.

Simultaneously, an attempt was made to keep the Buddhist monks disciplined and restricted in their activities by enforcing upon them their own monastic rules: the Vinaya. If stringently enforced, these detailed and rigid rules would have severely restricted proselytizing by the clergy and outlawed many of the economic enterprises from which the temples derived their wealth. It was no accident that the Sui founder chose a Vinaya master as official head of the Buddhist communities of the realm. And when he said to him "We, your disciple, are a lay Son of Heaven, while you, Vinaya Master, are a religious Son of Heaven," his words were not meant as a flowery compliment.[2] Rather they expressed his wish that this specialist in the monastic rules should take full responsibility for controlling and disciplining the clergy of the whole realm. The history of Buddhism in the T'ang suggests that such measures were only partly effective, for temples and temple wealth grew, often with the powerful and interested support of the empresses and their families, or of merchant groups who saw the Mahayana emphasis on the productive use of gift funds as a rationale for commercial enterprise, which was not otherwise en-

---

[2] Cf. *Hsü Kao-seng chuan*, ch. 21, *Taishō*, L, 610.

couraged in a political economy officially centered on agriculture.[3]

In addition to these official attempts to control Buddhist clergy and establishments, the Sui and T'ang governments were watchful for signs of subversive groups or doctrines among the Buddhists, particularly in the countryside, where officially approved clergy were scarce. Mahayana Buddhism had several doctrines that were of great potential usefulness to demagogues, rebels, or would-be usurpers. One was the doctrine of the three ages or periods of Buddhism, the last culminating in the extinction of the religion: once mankind was well into this last age—and certain signs indicated it was —there could be no government worthy of the respect and loyalty of the devout. Such a notion was utterly subversive, and when it was spread widely by such a wealthy and powerful sect as the San-chieh chiao, the Sui and T'ang governments repeatedly ordered the sect suppressed. Almost equally dangerous were the worshipers of Maitreya, the future Buddha, who believed that the end of the world was at hand, that the descent of Maitreya would inaugurate a new heaven and a new earth. The north in the period of disunion had seen numerous popular uprisings centered on this cult, and the Sui and T'ang governments were plagued by many more. In this and later periods, white—the color associated with Maitreya—figured prominently in the symbolism and ideologies of rebel movements.

Yet the occasional misgivings and the sporadic restrictive measures of the T'ang rulers were more than offset by the

[3] Gernet, *Aspects économiques* . . . , pp. 269–72.

religious devotion of their subjects. For the first two hundred years of the T'ang, Buddhism flourished as never before. Supported by the lavish donations of the devout, guided by leaders of true piety and brilliance, graced by the most gifted artists and architects of the age, Buddhism was woven into the very texture of Chinese life and thought. These centuries were the golden age of an independent and creative Chinese Buddhism.

Buddhist ritual now became an integral part of state and imperial observances. The accession of a new emperor, the birth of an imperial prince, ceremonies in honor of the imperial ancestors—all these occasions and many more now involved Buddhist rituals, the chanting of sutras and spells, maigre feasts for the clergy, ceremonial donations to temples and monasteries. The Sui and T'ang emperors had reestablished the Son of Heaven as the center and pivot of a reunited empire. But unlike their Han predecessors, whose position had been rationalized in the ideas and symbols of native traditions, these monarchs relied heavily on an alien religion to augment the credenda and miranda of their power.

In the artistic and cultural life of the great capital at Ch'ang-an, Buddhism was omnipresent. The gilded finials of innumerable temples and pagodas, the tolling of temple bells, the muted chanting of sutras, the passing to and fro of solemn processions were the palpable signs of Buddhism's ramifying influence in the life of the empire. The pagodas and the temple compounds testified to the long, slow blending of Indian and native elements into a new Sino-Buddhist architecture, whose glories we see reflected today in the buildings of the Hōryūji monastery in Japan. The images and paintings which filled the great buildings were, similarly, a culminating fusion of elements from the native tradition and elements from Indian, Persian, Greco-Roman, and Central Asian sources. The Buddhas and Bodhisattvas who looked down from their pedestals on congregations of the devout had Chinese faces with expressions of calm compassion which were distinctively Chinese translations of the Buddhist vision of life and time. In some the lines of the garments reflected Chinese taste and modes, but the ornaments and the gestures were taken from the iconography of Indian Buddhism. But this was selective. Surviving objects make it clear that the Chinese Buddhist artists and architects were by now emancipated from the authority of alien models and were creating a distinctively Chinese Buddhist art.

Of the officials and scholars of the prosperous empires of Sui and T'ang, some turned to Buddhism because of the appeal of its ideas or of its promise of salvation; others, more casually, were attracted by the aesthetic charm of its ceremonies and its superb temples. The famous poets and essayists who made the T'ang one of the great ages of Chinese literature were all familiar with Buddhist ideas, though many drew inspiration from a Taoism enriched by its Buddhist borrowings. In their poems one finds reflections of the public and private Buddhist observances which punctuated their lives, images and allusions drawn from their favorite Buddhist scriptures, descriptions of the lovely temples to which they often retreated for contemplation and converse with some noted monk. Po Chü-i evokes for us the atmosphere of a great monastery which he visited in 814:

> Straight before me were many Treasure Towers,
> Whose wind-bells at the four corners sang.
> At door and window, cornice and architrave
> A thick cluster of gold and green-jade.
>
> . . . .
>
> To the east there opens the Jade Image Hall,
> Where white Buddhas sit like serried trees.
> We shook from our garments the journey's grime and
>   dust,
> And bowing worshipped those faces of frozen snow
> Whose white cassocks like folded hoar-frost hung,
> Whose beaded crowns glittered like a shower of hail.
> We looked closer; surely Spirits willed
> This handicraft, never chisel carved![4]

If Buddhism permeated the life of the capital and the lives of the elite, it was hardly less prevalent in the towns and villages of the empire. A network of official temples linked provincial Buddhism to that of the imperial capital and reminded people through periodic rituals that this religion was the common faith of all Chinese. Officials taking up their local duties showed special marks of favor to the Buddhist clergy and establishments in their new districts. In addition there were innumerable privately endowed temples, often with extensive lands, mills, and regular fairs, which figured largely in the economic and social life of the countryside. In such temples the great days were the festi-

---

[4] Arthur Waley, *Chinese Poems* (London, 1946), p. 143.

vals of the Buddhist year, notably the Buddha's birthday and the Feast of All Souls, and crowds would gather on set occasions to pay homage to Buddhist deities, hear sutra readings, or listen to a noted preacher expound the doctrine. Local organizations of the faithful (*i-hui*) met frequently for vegetarian feasts, at which local clergy and laity joined in friendly intercourse; these associations attracted local residents to their meetings, enlisted them in the competition of gift-giving, and thus helped to spread Buddhism in the countryside.

The village clergy, though often not formally trained or officially ordained, knew their parishioners intimately. They officiated at marriages and funerals, and in general served the villagers not only as soothsayers and healers, but also—with their magical tricks and store of edifying tales— as entertainers. In many such functions they replaced the shamans and exorcists who had ministered to these needs in earlier times.[5] In humble villages, the Japanese pilgrim Ennin tells us, people of simple faith offered alms and hospitality to itinerant monks and to pilgrims traveling to the famous Buddhist shrines.[6] Often these shrines were located on mountains which in earlier ages had been centers for the cult of local tutelary divinities. Here, as in other ancient holy places, Buddhism was grafted onto indigenous cults, and Buddhist divinities gradually replaced the native gods. From Ennin's vivid and circumstantial account one can visualize the Buddhism of T'ang China as it affected the

---

[5] Gernet, *Aspects économiques* . . . , pp. 240–68.

[6] On popular Buddhism, cf. Edwin Reischauer's valuable study, *Ennin's Travels in T'ang China* (New York, 1955), pp. 164–216.

daily lives of the mighty and the humble, as it spread its symbols and its cults into every corner of the empire. One also sees in concrete detail the ways in which it worked as a social cement, binding together all classes and races in common beliefs and activities.

Such a common faith might be expected to have a wide influence on institutions and patterns of behavior. For example, Buddhist teachings of compassion and respect for life should have done much to moderate the cruel punishments decreed in Chinese penal codes. There are at least scattered indications that it did. Thus, in the Sui and T'ang periods imperial amnesties and particularly the remission of death sentences were justified partly in Buddhist terms. And these dynasties, continuing the Buddhist customs of earlier regimes, forbade executions or the killing of any living thing during the first, fifth, and ninth months—periods of Buddhist abstinence.[7]

Ironically, Buddhism was also used by the state for the psychological conditioning of its armies. The Chinese cult of filial piety had had a chilling effect on martial ardor. It laid upon every man a heavy obligation to return his body intact upon his death and thus to show gratitude to his parents who had given it to him; there was the further teaching that the only immortality a man could expect was the honor paid him by his descendants in the family graveyard and ancestral temple. Warriors thus had a horror of a disfiguring death in battle and of burial far from home. The Chinese Buddhist conception of a soul brought with it a new notion

---

[7] Cf. *T'ang hui-yao* (Commercial Press edition), ch. 41, p. 733.

of immortality, and the Sui and T'ang dynasties made a practice of building battlefield temples at the scenes of major engagements and endowing perpetual services for the repose of the souls of the war dead and their ultimate salvation.

More significantly, the growth of Buddhism as a common faith was accompanied by a great increase in charitable works of all kinds. Buddhist monks had been the first to open free dispensaries, and in time of epidemics the clergy ministered to thousands in the stricken areas. They established free hospitals, to which, by T'ang times, the state was contributing support. Buddhist congregations supported the chains of free or low-cost hostels reported by Ennin, and such charitable enterprises as the building of bridges and the planting of shade trees along well-traveled roads.

The nature and scale of these undertakings suggest two ways in which Buddhism wrought profound changes in Chinese society. One was by opposing a universal ethic to the long-prevailing familism and particularism of indigenous traditions. The other, linked to this, was by propagating the idea of the spiritual debt and the expiatory gift. As Gernet has observed, gifts to a pious activity—a contribution to the welfare of living creatures—were believed to reduce the burden of evil karma from past lives and to expiate recent acts of self-interest on the part of the donor. The self-immolating monks who emulated the Bodhisattvas by literally giving all for the benefit of all provided the model and the inspiration for the giving of gifts. The poor were thus moved to give a few copper cash or some of their few possessions, while the wealthy often donated lands, the income from which would provide a continuous flow of expiatory gifts and thus contribute to their eternal spiritual felicity. Yet it would be mistaken to suppose that the universalistic ethic of Buddhism simply replaced the old Chinese family feeling; rather, as we saw in the Buddhist inscriptions of the period of disunion, donations for pious works continued to be qualified by provisions for special attention to the welfare of the donor's family and clan. As we shall see, this blend of Buddhist ethical universalism and Chinese ethical particularism eventually became a part of the new Confucianism which began to develop in the tenth century.

We now turn to the great Buddhist movements which arose in response to the needs of Chinese society in the Sui and T'ang, and in turn shaped the evolving patterns of Chinese Buddhist thought and behavior. These movements were built upon the deepened knowledge of Buddhism which the great translators and spiritual leaders of earlier centuries had made possible. Despite the ultimate Indian origin of their ideas and practices, these movements were unmistakably Chinese. To be sure, the greatest T'ang translators and exegetists — the great pilgrim-translator Hsüan-tsang is an outstanding example—learned Sanskrit and were not dependent on Chinese translations and commentaries for their comprehension of Buddhist doctrine. Yet Sanskrit never became a "church language" as Latin did in the West; Chinese Buddhists with such linguistic knowledge were a tiny minority, and most, if not all, of the seminal thinkers and founders of schools of Chinese Buddhism knew only Chinese. Further, there was no Rome or al-Azhar to provide a center of orthodoxy, a check on the doctrinal innovations of Buddhist thinkers throughout southern and eastern Asia. In short, the Buddhist schools and movements of this period are fully intelligible only in the light of the traditions and long-run tendencies of Chinese thought, and the spiritual and intellectual needs of the Chinese people of the time.

In the thought and writings of all the schools there are emphases, modes of expression, and interpretations which have no Indian analogue. For example, Indian abstractions almost invariably came to be expressed in concrete images. We find "perfection" rendered as *yüan*, "round"; "essence" explained as *yen-mu*, "the eye," or *yen-ching*, "the pupil of the eye"; "one's true nature" referred to as *pen-lai mien-mu*, "original face and eyes."[8] A complex of abstractions was likely to be explained diagramatically; a chain sequence of abstract propositions was often reduced to a series of more or less concrete metaphors.[9] Few of the innovations in Chinese Buddhist thought in this period of independent growth were systematic extensions of Indian ideas. Rather they were reinterpretations, restatements of these ideas through typically Chinese modes of thought and expression.

The school of meditation, Ch'an in Chinese, Zen in Japanese, was one of the most influential schools, with a particular appeal to the Chinese elite. Although the full maturity of Ch'an Buddhism dates from the T'ang, its origins as a school go back at least to the sixth century, and

---

[8] Examples drawn from Hajime Nakamura, *Tōyōjin no shi-i hō-hō* ("Modes of thought of East Asian peoples") (Tokyo, 1948), I, 348 ff.

[9] *Ibid.*

its central doctrines—that the Buddha-nature is immanent in all beings, and that its discovery through meditation and introspection brings release from illusion—go back even further. As we have seen, these doctrines were prefigured in the philosophical discussions of the fourth century.

So also was the controversy over the process of enlightment, which in the T'ang period divided Ch'an into two main branches. In this controversy one branch held that enlightment came in a single moment of sudden and total illumination, the other that it came about in the course of a long, many-phased program of discipline and meditation. The subitist branch of Ch'an had closer affinities with the native tradition of Taoism, but both branches can best be understood as complex amalgams of Buddhist and Taoist ideas. The distrust of words, the rich store of concrete metaphor and analogy, the love of paradox, the bibliophobia, the belief in the direct, person-to-person, and often wordless communication of insight, the feeling that life led in close communion with nature is conducive to enlightenment —all these are colored with Taoism. Indeed Ch'an may be regarded as the reaction of a powerful tradition of Chinese thought against the verbosity, the scholasticism, the tedious logical demonstrations, of the Indian Buddhist texts. And, in its subitist branch, which became dominant, it asserts an ideal of salvation that echoes the persisting Chinese belief— alien to caste-bound India—that a man may, in his lifetime, rise to the heights through his own efforts.[10] In the Confucian tradition this is expressed in the saying "Anyone can become a sage like Yao or Shun," and in Taoism in stories

---

[10] Jacques Gernet, *Entretiens du maître de Dhyāna Chen-Houei de Ho-tsö* (Hanoi, 1949), p. iv.

of unlettered artisans whose grasp of the *tao* surpassed that of their social betters.

The school of Ch'an, with its sophisticated philosophy of intuition, its intense concentration on individual enlightenment, and its sense of the *tao* or Buddha-nature immanent in nature, had an irresistible appeal for artists, writers, and all those who, for longer or shorter periods, sought the life of contemplation. The T'ang poets often refer to their retreats in Ch'an temples or their conversations with Ch'an masters. From time to time Ch'an Buddhism attracted the favor and patronage of a sympathetic emperor, and in the T'ang it became established as a Buddhist school with a strong and enduring attraction for the educated elite; we shall see that its influence persisted long after other schools of Buddhism declined.

A school with a different emphasis was the T'ien-t'ai, named for the mountain in Chekiang where its founder Chih-i (531–97) established its principal temple. Chih-i, like many other Chinese Buddhists, was deeply troubled by the multiplicity of Buddhist doctrines and by the contradictory teachings found in Buddhist texts of diverse periods and origins. He developed what might be called a syncretism on historical principles. By this I mean that he set up a doctrine of the levels of Buddhist teachings, with each level corresponding to a phase in the life of the Buddha and to the sort of clientele he was speaking to in that phase. For Chih-i it followed that each level of the doctrine—each approach to Buddhist truth—had its peculiar validity; the ultimate or all-encompassing doctrine was that found in the Lotus sutra.

T'ien-t'ai Buddhism, though its ritual, its iconography,

and its psychological regimen are of Indian Buddhist origin, is distinctively Chinese in several respects. It reflects the perennial Chinese effort to reconcile divergent views, itself perhaps a reflection of the high valuation assigned by the Chinese to harmony in human affairs. Its primary means of reconciliation—a sort of historical relativism—dates back to the classical philosophies of the Chou period. By reason of this formula for the reduction of doctrinal friction, T'ient'ai understandably had a strong appeal to the reunifying dynasty of Sui. It continued to flourish in the T'ang; its appeal, then and later, was largely to the literate class.

There were other schools that represented certain positions in a spectrum of philosophic choices or commitments to the authority of particular texts. Like the schools of Chinese philosophy, few of them were dogmatic or exclusive, and it was usual for a Chinese intellectual to move from one to another as his interests changed. Many such schools were of limited appeal and relatively short-lived. What is important, however, is not that some schools flourished while others languished, but rather that Buddhism in one form or another met most of the intellectual and spiritual needs of the upper class. Ch'an Buddhism offered a morally strengthened, intellectually deepened continuation of the tradition of philosophic Taoism, while other schools offered modes of scholarship and self-cultivation plus an enlarged vision of time, human nature, and destiny that were far more satisfying than the fragmented and by now archaistic Confucian tradition.

The activities of Buddhist schools, for all their influence on philosophy, aesthetics, literature, and art, would not fully account for the changes in the pattern of life, in common attitudes and values, that we described earlier in this chapter. Faith, belief in the saving power of Buddhas and Bodhisattvas, had gradually come to pervade all classes of Chinese society, and it lay behind all the new patterns of individual and group behavior we have mentioned, from the monk's spectacular self-immolation to the peasant's meager offering before some rural shrine. Consideration of the nature of this faith as it found expression in various schools, sects, and cults should dispose of a quite baseless myth that has long beclouded discussions of religion in China: the notion that the Chinese are rationalistic and ethnocentric and thus somehow immune to religious emotion. We have only to confront this myth with the great surge of religious feeling behind the Yellow Turban uprising of the second century, or the fanaticism of Chinese converts to Islam or lately to Communism, and it is apparent that the Chinese capacity for commitment to a saving faith is strong and persisting. Salvationist Buddhism in this period of independent growth is neither an anomaly nor a temporary aberration of an otherwise "rational" people.

The notion that the compassionate Bodhisattvas could intervene in the lives of men to save them from danger, to help them to felicity, and—above all—to guide them to bliss beyond the grave, was present in numerous texts of the Mahayana. It was popularized for the common people in the sermons of lay and clerical preachers, in tales of the Bodhisattvas' saving interventions, in forged popular "sutras" written to Chinese tastes, and in collections of cases of the working of karmic retribution and divine grace.

Each of the many Buddhist deities presided over a heaven which was colorfully and appealingly described and contrasted with the torments of innumerable hells. Devotion to Maitreya, the future Buddha, who would waft believers to his heaven to await the new and better age over which he would preside, was gradually superseded by the cult of Amitābha (Chinese O-mi-t'o-fo, Japanese Amida), who rewarded the faithful with rebirth in his western paradise. This was to prove the most enduring of the popular faiths. Two lesser T'ang cults—those of Kuan-yin (Avalokiteśvara) and Wen-chu-shih-li (Mañjusri), each with his peculiar powers and promises of salvation—were very widespread in their time. Of a slightly different order was belief in the power of the Lotus sutra, whose invocation, recitation, or reproduction would ameliorate worldly ills and ensure happiness beyond the grave. Still another manifestation of Buddhist fervor was the adoration of certain relics of the Buddha and of the saints which were enshrined in temples in the capital and in the provinces.

In contrast to the shadowy "immortals" of religious Taoism and its psycho-physical regimens, Buddhism offered a rich iconography and mythology which would fire even the most sluggish imagination. In place of the nature spirits and tutelary divinities of an earlier time, Buddhism offered gods of great color and warmth, magnificent ceremonies replete with music and symbolism, and spiritual rewards undreamed of in the older religions.

By the eighth century, Buddhism was fully and triumphantly established throughout China. Its canons were revered, its spiritual truth unquestioned. It marked and influenced the lives of the humble and the great and affected every community, large and small, in the empire of T'ang. What then accounts for its slow decline from the late ninth century onward? Many factors were at work—in the next chapter I shall elaborate on those I believe to have been decisive. The decline of Buddhism in India meant that the flow of new ideas into China gradually dwindled and, with the eleventh century, ceased altogether. In the years 755–63 the great T'ang empire was wracked by the rebellion of An Lu-shan—a rebellion which resulted in the humiliation of the ruling house, the impoverishment of the country, and, indirectly, the growth of centers of power in the provinces that further weakened the dynasty. The rebellion and its aftermath weakened T'ang self-confidence, and the cosmopolitanism of the great days of the dynasty gave way to a cultural defensiveness which occasionally turned into xenophobia. Finally, there were threats from Central Asia and repeated interventions by Uighurs and Turks in the affairs of the weakened empire.

The old and oft-repeated attacks on Buddhism now had a more receptive hearing than heretofore. The charge of being foreign in origin and an *imperium in imperio*, the accusation of wasteful expenditure on temples, images, and ceremonies, strictures against the idleness of the clergy and the tax-exempt status of Buddhist lands — these charges, which two hundred years before had found not a single supporter at the T'ang court, now became the basis of policy and action. The upshot was the great suppression of Buddhism between 842 and 845, which brought empire-wide destruction of temples and shrines, confiscation of Buddhist lands, and secularization of the clergy. Although Buddhism was later allowed to revive, this suppression, together with certain social changes dating from the eighth century, greatly undermined its vitality. Jacques Gernet describes these changes and their effects in this way:

> What gave strength to the religious movement at its height is its extension through the whole of Chinese society and the multiplicity of religious clienteles and groups: disciples of the great monks, peasants attached to the monasteries and incorporated into the Sangha [The Buddhist Church], the followers of the monks belonging to the great families, communities patronized by notable people; this is the communion which brought about the great common observances among opposing classes and the religious association which brought together monks, influential families, and common people. . . . But a profound change in these traditional structures took place in the course of the eighth century, the century which in our view clearly marked a turning point in the history of Chinese Buddhism. One observes then the formation of a class of farmers and agricultural workers. This historical phenomenon can be considered as at once a symptom and a cause of a new conception of social relations. Thereafter there were employers and employees, and in the fiscal realm the tendency was toward a money economy. One can legitimately link the individual drive to profit with a more and more accentuated isolation of the social classes one from another. Buddhism, in developing its followings, had adapted itself to the old structures. Their ruin had a dissolving effect on a religious phenomenon which drew its strength from its universality.[11]

---

[11] Gernet, *Aspects économiques* . . . , p. 298.

Still more important, perhaps, was the revival—under the impact of the historical forces just described—of the native tradition of Confucianism by an important segment of the Chinese elite. This revival, in my view, marked the beginning of the end of Buddhist influence among the literate, and may properly be regarded as the first phase of the long process of appropriation with which the next chapter will be concerned.

CHAPTER FIVE

THE PERIOD OF APPROPRIATION

Long before the ninth century, as we have seen, the Sui and T'ang dynasties took official action to restore a Confucianism which had been largely eclipsed in the period of disunion. This revival was a selective one, shaped and limited by the political interests of the ruling houses; its principal institutional expression was an examination system, designed to provide a more broadly based officialdom than earlier dynasties—many of them virtually the captives of a few aristocratic families—had enjoyed. The examination system was inevitably established with a Confucian curriculum, despite the generally strong Taoist or Buddhist sympathies of the Sui and T'ang rulers, because Confucianism provided the only available corpus of political theory, ritual precedents, and normative rules for the conduct of court and official affairs. The Confucian classics, carefully re-edited and provided with the officially approved commentaries of K'ung Ying-ta (574–647), formed the core of the new curriculum. Ambitious young men of good family were thus provided with orthodox interpretations which they could memorize and apply to the stereotyped questions set by the examiners.

The limitations of this Sui and T'ang revival are significant. Confucian learning, it is true, was now the passport to office and wealth, and was imposed on aspiring youths of the literate class. But the new orthodox commentaries were sober, rather pedantic siftings of available interpretations and were in no sense a recasting or updating of Confucian thought as a whole. Thus those who studied for the examinations were rather bored than inspired by their studies, and the examination questions themselves were stilted scholastic or literary exercises rather than challenges to the creative intellect. As a result the focus of intellectual interest remained, until the ninth century, in the alien tradition of Buddhism. At the same time a knowledge of the basic texts and ideas of Confucianism was widespread, and when the historical factors mentioned earlier began to work against Buddhism, there was a shared body of knowledge among the literati which could conceivably provide the basis for a thoroughgoing revival and recasting of the indigenous tradition.

In the years of the An Lu-shan catastrophe and its aftermath, men of learning and conscience turned with a new seriousness to the Confucian canon. They sought in it ways to diagnose the crisis of their time and formulas for its solution. They were critical of the official commentaries and of the skeins of literary artifice and allusive rhetoric that convention demanded in the examinations and, indeed, in all serious writing. These men, whose gropings anticipate the full-scale Confucian revival, were generally not opposed to Buddhism, nor did they identify themselves as the chosen instruments for a sweeping overhaul of the existing order.[1]

It was Han Yü (786–824)—a brilliant polemicist and an ardent xenophobe—who pulled together the criticisms made by his older contemporaries and laid down the formula for cultural renaissance: Purge Chinese tradition of all the noxious accretions of the years of Buddhist dominance; return directly to the immortal truths laid down by the Chinese sages; rally all men of good will and build a new order on those truths. Many of his contemporaries regarded him as crude and intemperate, but his program prefigured the revival that was to come. The eleventh-century scholar Ou-yang Hsiu stated more fully and presciently the shape which the revival was to take.

In his *Pen-lun* Ou-yang reviews the Buddhist penetration of China and attributes it—correctly, I think—to a general weakening of Chinese institutions, though his idealized view of pre-Buddhist antiquity is the product of emotional commitment rather than historical judgment. He admits that the task of revitalizing Confucianism is not easy: "This curse [Buddhism] has overspread the empire for a thousand years, and what can one man in one day do about it? The people are drunk with it, and it has entered the marrow of their bones; it is surely not to be overcome by eloquent talk. What, then, is to be done?" Concluding that the only solution is to correct the "root cause" of the evil, he presents the historical examples which should be a guide in this process:

---

[1] See Edwin Pulleyblank, "On the Intellectual History of the Yüan-ho Period." To appear in A. F. Wright, ed., *The Confucian Persuasion* (Stanford, 1959).

Of old, in the time of the Warring States, Yang Chu and Mo Ti were engaged in violent controversy. Mencius deplored this and devoted himself to teaching benevolence and righteousness. His exposition of benevolence and righteousness won the day, and the teachings of Yang Chu and Mo Ti were extirpated. In Han times the myriad schools of thought all flourished together. Tung Chung-shu deplored this and revived Confucianism. Therefore the Way of Confucius shone forth, and the myriad schools expired. This is the effect of what I have called "correcting the root cause in order to overcome the evil."[2]

It is Ou-yang Hsiu's invocation of the example of Tung Chung-shu that is striking here. For, as we noted earlier, Tung "revived"—we would say reformulated—Confucianism in the Han by incorporating in his new synthesis the doctrines of rival schools that challenged Confucian dominance. And this is precisely the way in which the reviving Confucianism of the eleventh century dealt with the competing traditions of Buddhism and Taoism. This second major recasting of Confucianism, like the first, occurred when political and social change had brought new problems which neither Buddhism nor an archaic Confucianism was equipped to deal with. We shall touch on some aspects of the changed society of Sung China later in this chapter.

The revived Confucianism of the Sung—the body of thought which Westerners call neo-Confucianism—is basically social and ethical in its interests. As de Bary has shown, its early formulators were men dedicated to the fundamen-

---

[2] See Ou-yang Hsiu's *Pen-lun. Ssu-pu ts'ung-k'an*, Series I, CXCIII, 150.

tal reform of outworn institutions, to the creation of a new ethos in a new society.[3] This meant that they were bitterly opposed to the otherworldliness, the antisocial values which they associated with Buddhism. And they somehow convinced themselves and others that the intrusion of Buddhism had turned Chinese thought and society away from the infallible norms laid down by the sages of antiquity. They therefore felt that their mission was to purify Chinese thought and behavior of this alien dross. Yet they proved to be in many ways the captives of the tradition they sought to replace. Chu Hsi, the authoritative formulator of neo-Confucianism, saw Buddhism as the enemy, yet he was concerned with winning over the intelligentsia of his time to his new doctrine; to this end he was bound to deal with the whole range of philosophic problems which Buddhism had raised and to provide non-Buddhist solutions for them.[4] Thus he developed in his thought a cosmology, a set of metaphysical notions, a cluster of psychological concepts, that would have been incomprehensible to Confucius or Tung Chung-shu but that were both comprehensible and appealing to his contemporaries with their Buddhist backgrounds and interests. The molders of neo-Confucianism lived in a climate suffused with Buddhist influence. Even the language and the modes of discourse at their disposal had developed in the ages of Buddhist dominance. The new dimensions of meaning which they discovered in the

[3] W. Theodore de Bary, "A Reappraisal of Neo-Confucianism," in Arthur F. Wright, ed., *Studies in Chinese Thought* (Chicago, 1953), pp. 81–111.

[4] Cf. Galen E. Sargent, *Tchou Hi contre le Bouddhisme* (Paris, 1955), p. 7 and *passim*.

ancient Chinese classics were dimensions which experience with Buddhism had taught them to seek and to find.

Thus in many of the key concepts of the new formulations one can see clearly the cumulative effect of the Buddhist experience. For example, in the dichotomy of *li*, principle, and *ch'i*, matter, the pre-Buddhist meaning of *li* as merely rational order has been replaced by a notion of *li* as a pan-absolute in the Mahayana Buddhist mode, akin, as Demiéville suggests, to the "One" in neo-Platonism. Neo-Confucianism opposed *li* to *ch'i* very much as Buddhism had come to oppose *li* and *shih*, absolute principle and facts or events.[5]

If the neo-Confucianism of Chu Hsi and his successors—with its emphasis on the slow accumulation of knowledge of the supreme principle and its manifestations in phenomena, understanding, and moral perfection—had been the only school of neo-Confucianism, it might have left Buddhism with a following among those who were attracted to introspection and intuition as paths to understanding and self-realization. For more than two centuries after Chu Hsi, those interested in these paths to enlightment continued to turn to Ch'an Buddhism, and Ch'an remained a major influence in literature and the arts. Eventually, however, it was challenged by a second variety of neo-Confucianism, which stressed, as Ch'an Buddhism had done, the direct apprehension of ultimate reality through meditation upon that segment of ultimate reality which is within. Wang Yangming (1472–1529), who gave this new doctrine its fullest

---

[5] Demiéville, "La Pénétration . . . ," p. 31.

formulation, also provided prescriptions for behavior that made his teachings explicitly relevant to the active careers of the scholar-official class. Wang's enemies called him a Buddhist in disguise, but the "disguise" was all-important in an age when the Chinese were turning away from an alien tradition and ransacking their own to find viable substitutes for Buddhist ideas.

In effect, then, two traditions of neo-Confucianism can be correlated with the two paths to understanding and self-knowledge that had developed in the controversies of the age of Buddhist dominance. The school of Chu Hsi represented the gradualist tendency; the school of Wang Yang-ming represented the subitist. These were the chief ways in which Buddhist ideas were appropriated by a reinvigorated Confucianism, with the result that Buddhist philosophy gradually lost ground to its native rivals as a focus of intellectual interest.

Neo-Confucianism, if it had been simply a "philosophy" in the Western sense, could not have achieved the dominance over Chinese life and institutions which it maintained until only yesterday. Its strength lay in the comprehensiveness of its prescriptions for the conduct of group and individual life, in its provision of formulas for government and social control, in its standards of aesthetic and moral judgment. In these facets of neo-Confucianism as they were reflected in policy and behavior, one sees again the pervasive influence of ideals appropriated from Buddhism.

Among the social reformers and statesmen of the Sung and after, one finds a strain of idealism, a heightened social conscience that had been missing in the stale archaism of

T'ang Confucian scholarship. This is to be seen in the reform programs of Fan Chung-yen (989–1052), Wang An-shih (1021–86), and their successors in later times. It was Fan Chung-yen who introduced the new ideal of the Confucian scholar, "one who is first in worrying about the world's troubles and last in enjoying its pleasures." As James Liu remarks, "This maxim became an article of political faith deeply imprinted in the mind of the scholar class. As recently as a decade ago, it was often assigned as an essay topic in modern schools."[6] This element of ethical universalism which found expression in the new Confucianism was appropriated from Mahayana Buddhism. It cast in secular Chinese terms the Bodhisattva ideal so eloquently stated by Sāntideva: "May I become an unfailing store for the wretched and be first to supply them with the manifold things of their need. My own self and my pleasures, all my righteousness, past, present, and future, I sacrifice without regard, in order to achieve the welfare of all beings."[7]

This awakened social conscience was reflected in the sphere of practical action. The Sung dynasty, during which neo-Confucianism was first formulated, was notable for its works of charity and relief. In contrast to the T'ang, during which charitable works were largely in the hands of pious families or of temples and religious organizations, the Sung

---

[6] See James T. C. Liu, "An Early Sung Reformer: Fan Chung-yen," in John K. Fairbank, ed., *Chinese Thought and Institutions* (Chicago, 1957), pp. 105–31. The passage cited, p. 111.

[7] Sāntideva's *Bodhicaryāvatāra*, translated in E. J. Thomas, *The History of Buddhist Thought* (London, 1933), p. 197. The Bodhisattva ideal was stated and elaborated in innumerable Buddhist texts. See, for example, Hsüan-tsang's translation of the *Abhidharmakośa, Taishō*, XXIX, 64.

measures were initiated and administered by the govern-ment. Imperial decrees ordered the maintenance at state expense of public clinics, of an empire-wide system of homes for the aged, the infirm, and the orphaned, and of public cemeteries. It is true that Buddhist monks were given official appointments as managers of many of these enterprises, but the initiative came from neo-Confucian officials.[8] In a sense the Buddhist idea of compassion and many of the measures developed for its practical expression had been appropriated by the Chinese state.

This Confucianism with new intellectual content, new ideals of individual and group behavior, and new formulas for institutional life was propagated by increasingly effective governmental machinery in a society which was undergoing great changes. To these changes we shall now turn our at-tention.

The society of the Sung dynasty and after, in which Buddhism was increasingly appropriated by native tradi-tions and progressively weakened, was a far different society from that of the T'ang. The great families which had been patrons of Buddhism for many generations were gone for-ever, and there was now greater social mobility than ever before. Great unwalled cities, the centers of an expanding commercial and industrial life, produced new wealth and new families aspiring to power. The last frontiers were closing, and rural gentry families rose and fell as they vied in the purchase and exploitation of available land. Thus an

---

[8] Cf. Hsü I-t'ang, "Social Relief during the Sung Dynasty" translated by E-tu Zen Sun and John de Francis in *Chinese Social History* (Washington, 1956), pp. 207–15.

ever-increasing number of candidates from a greater number of literate families competed in the great civil service examinations, for which they studied the orthodox neo-Confucian teachings of Chu Hsi.

Printing, whose invention was closely associated with Buddhism, now made it possible for more and more people to study the neo-Confucian texts and thus prepare for the examinations. The spread of both public and private academies in the Sung and after brought neo-Confucian ideas to communities throughout the empire. No Buddhist temple or monastery was now far away from a secular center which propagated the new Confucianism both as a body of ideas and as a passport to wealth and power. As a result, men of wealth were more apt to contribute to the foundation of an academy than to the upkeep of a temple or cult; men of quality gradually ceased to consider the Buddhist priesthood a worthy career for themselves or their sons. Inevitably many of the once great and imposing temples fell into ruins. An eighteenth-century poet captures for us the atmosphere of one of these abandoned temples:

> No monk lives at the old temple, the Buddha has
>   toppled to the floor;
> One bell hangs high, bright with evening sun.
> Sad that when only a tap is needed, no one now
>   dares
> To rouse the notes of solemn music that cram
>   its ancient frame.[9]

The gradual turning away from Buddhism was not

---

[9] Arthur Waley, *Yuan Mei, An Eighteenth Century Poet* (London, 1956), p. 102. This poem, entitled "The Bell," was written in 1769.

wholly the result of the intellectual and spiritual competition offered by neo-Confucianism and of the social incentives provided by the examination system. It should be emphasized that the dynasties which ruled China from the Sung until 1912 developed a far more elaborate and effective apparatus for imposing an official orthodoxy than earlier regimes. In addition to the highly organized examination system there was increasing official control over all school curricula, government censorship and suppression of deviationist or subversive writings, a network of controls that reached more aspects of private life and thought than government had ever before attempted to influence.

The new Confucianism provided the elite with a philosophy and ideology in which those elements of Buddhist thought with a continuing appeal had been unconsciously appropriated. This involved, as we have noted, the gradual withdrawal of upper-class interest and patronage from traditions of Buddhist thought whose inner vitality had begun to wane; it also involved the development of a pattern of life in which Buddhist ideas and observances had scant place. The new thought, the new patterns of group and individual behavior which it rationalized, the access to power promised to its disciples—all gave elite life and thought a new unity and coherence. It was one of the sacred obligations of a Confucian monarch and a Confucian elite to spread orthodox doctrines throughout society, and in the period we are considering there was continuous pressure from government and officialdom to detach the masses from their religious ties and win them to the lay ethic of neo-Confucianism.

Yet all these factors combined did not transform the

peasant masses into sedate and rational, if impoverished, counterparts of their social betters. Religiosity remained high throughout this long period — witness the fanatical rebel movements, the countless local religious organizations, the rites of the secret societies, the continuous patronage of mediums, exorcists, and the cults of numberless divinities. In contrast to the earlier period in which Buddhism, in different forms, had formed a common bond between the two main classes of Chinese society, the modern period saw a striking cleavage between the rational ethic of the elite and the religious ethos of the peasantry. An astute observer has suggested that the two classes can be regarded as sub-societies, the upper being what Ruth Benedict called an Apollonian and the lower a Dionysiac.[10] To the degree that this is true, the appropriation of Buddhism in popular culture must be viewed as a separate process, affected, but seldom decisively, by government policies. Let us turn to some aspects of the appropriation of Buddhism at the popular level.

Here we should emphasize the importance of religious Taoism, whose borrowing of religious ideas, divinities, and cults from Buddhism had begun at least as early as the fifth century and continued at an accelerated pace throughout the next millennium. This was a formidable and flexible rival of popular Buddhism in the countryside. Unencumbered by the intellectual freight which Buddhism carried, popular Taoism was free to improvise divinities and cults whenever the need arose, and its particular strength lay in its ability

---

[10] Rolf Stein, "Les Religions de l'Orient et de l'extrême-Orient," in *L'Encyclopédie française*, XIX (Paris, 1957), 54–55.

to absorb or reabsorb local nature divinities and cults that had a history reaching back to pre-Buddhist times. Taoism's control of much of traditional medicine, and its virtual monopoly of the techniques of geomancy (which also incorporated Indian ideas) and divination, assured it of a regular clientele. What Sir Charles Eliot called the fluid polydaemonism of Chinese peasant religion worked for the steady absorption of Buddhist gods and cults by the native rival.

Ultimately Buddhist, Taoist, and folk-religious elements fused into an almost undifferentiated popular religion. The Buddhist pantheon was, in a sense, the victim of its own adaptability. It had been easy for a Buddha or a Bodhisattva to take on one or more attributes of a local god and replace him in the temple of the local cult. But now its originally Buddhist character was gradually obliterated as the god took on other attributes given him by his devotees. This Sinicization of the Buddhist pantheon began at least as early as the Sung dynasty. Alexander Soper describes some aspects of the process:

> The artists transformed the Bodhisattva type from a swart half-naked Indian to a more decently clad divinity with a properly light complexion; the faithful gave special honor to the figures in the pantheon who claimed personal connection with China. Popular imagination, beginning to express itself in Buddhist terms, created a whole new category of demi-gods, the Lo-han linked by name to the Arhats of India but more nearly kin to the picturesque Hsien, the mountain-dwelling, cloud-riding immortals of Taoism.[11]

---

[11] Alexander Soper, "Hsiang-kuo-ssu, an Imperial Temple of Northern Sung," *JAOS*, LXVIII (1948), 36.

1

2

3

4

5

6

7

8

Another force for Sinicization which we see at work on the Lo-han and other figures in the Buddhist pantheon is euhemerism—the tendency of a history-loving people to invest a god with the character and pedigree of a historical personality. Thus, for example, the Buddhist divinity Yama, King of Hell (Yen-lo in Chinese), became identified with a Sui dynasty official who died in A.D. 592.[12] Such changes in the pantheon were reflected in the iconography of Chinese Buddhism. By modern times the ascetic spirituality and the symbols of wisdom and salvation characteristic of earlier figures had disappeared. The Maitreyas, Amitābhas, and other divinities had been transformed from symbols of religious ideas and aspirations into the potbellied patrons of one earthly concern or another: pawnbroker guilds, local industry, expectant motherhood.

The Buddhists, as we have seen, had early adopted and maintained an Erastian position which ultimately gave the emperors wide powers not only over clergy and temples but over the pantheon itself. Gods could be promoted or demoted, given or deprived of attributes, by imperial order. In the period of appropriation, this imperial power was used with dissolving effects upon the Buddhist pantheon. Sometimes a deity of a rival faith—usually religious Taoism—was elevated to perform functions once attributed to a Buddhist divinity; thus the Emperor Hui-tsung in 1116 invested the Taoist divinity Yü-huang Shang-ti, the Jade Emperor, with wide powers in the nether world that had once been exercised by Buddhist divinities. Another case of a somewhat different

---

[12] Henri Maspero, "The Mythology of Modern China," in J. Hackin *et al.*, *Asiatic Mythology* (London, 1932), pp. 363–64.

order was that of the Taoist divinity Kuan-ti, the god of war, who in the last dynasty was officially given the title of Hu-kuo fo, "The Buddha who defends the realm."[13]

The power of the state was used in still another way to promote the fusion of popular religions. The aim of the state, when it realistically recognized that neo-Confucianism could not satisfy the religious needs of the peasantry, was to promote observances conducive to social conformity, good order, and harmony among the populace. There were occasional pious Buddhist emperors whose munificent patronage gave an autumnal splendor to the great temples, and the Manchu dynasty patronized Lamaistic Buddhism as an instrument of Inner Asian policy. But the policy of one ruler after another was to insist on the fusion of those beliefs and practices of all religions that tended to good order. The official view was that if elements of Buddhist belief retained an attraction for some and were conducive to social order, then let them exist in syncretic amalgam so that they would be tamed and modified by the dominant tradition of Confucianism. As early as the eleventh century a Buddhist monk had combined the worship of Confucius, Buddha, and Lao-tzu in a single cult, and many temples of the Sung and later periods had special halls for this worship. There were occasional official protests objecting that Confucius should properly be exalted over the other two, but the cult had a considerable popular following into the nineteenth century. The observations of a seventeenth-century official who con-

---

[13] Cf. Thomas Watters, *Essays on the Chinese Language* (Shanghai, 1889), p. 468. See also chaps. viii and ix of this work, "The Influence of Buddhism on the Chinese Language."

tributed to the repair of a local temple to the Three Teachings may serve to illustrate the selective and pragmatic view of Buddhism that was widespread among officialdom:

> I have examined carefully into the methods of the ancient rulers. When the people are at peace, they are governed and live according to the proper rules of conduct (*Li*), but when troubles arise, punishments must be used. When these penalties are not sufficient to control the people, the sanctions of religion must be employed, for men are frightened by spiritual forces which they cannot see nor hear. We know that Buddha lived in ancient times, and we may employ his teaching, with that of Lao Tzi, even though we do not use their names, to reinforce the doctrines of Confucius . . . Although the doctrines of the wheels of life (Karma and Salvation), of suffering and blessedness, were introduced to deceive the people, yet they were useful in frightening men, in awakening them to the necessity of right behavior, and in checking their sinful desires.[14]

As a result of all these tendencies and state policies, the humble worshiper at a local shrine was progressively less aware of the provenance of the deity to whom he addressed a special request. A 1948 report on the popular cults of one county reports that only 19.7 per cent of the local cult units were identifiably Buddhist, and a number of deities in these were tending to be confused with those of non-Buddhist origin.[15]

---

[14] Passage from the County Gazetteer (*hsien-chih*) of Anking, Anhwei, translated in John K. Shryock, *The Temples of Anking, and Their Cults* (Paris, 1931), pp. 132–33.

[15] William A. Grootaers, "Temples and History of Wan ch'üan, Chahar," *Monumenta Serica*, XIII (1948), 314. A total of 851 temples and shrines were studied.

The heavens and hells of Indian Buddhism were appropriated by the native popular religion of Taoism, and became in turn places for the reward or retribution of accumulated karma that were characteristic of an undifferentiated folk religion. In this process of appropriation, the heavens and hells retained some of the delights and torments that had been the product of Indian imagination, but the Taoist tradition endowed them with a bureaucratic structure that was unmistakably Chinese. The deities of the various nether worlds became a bureaucracy with a table of organization, offices for the keeping of voluminous records, bureaus with functional responsibilities, and so forth. The popular Sino-Buddhist view of the after-life is revealed in a typical story of a peasant woman. After her death, her family inquired through a medium (not a Buddhist monk) about her status in the nether world. She replied through the medium that she had now expiated her evil karma and had applied to the proper authorities for reincarnation in human form, that her papers were in order, and that she expected an early decision.[16] Here the Buddhist idea of karma is still recognizable, but the structure of the nether world and the desideratum of rebirth as a human being are wholly and typically Chinese.

In popular festivals the same process of appropriation is to be observed. Buddhist elements are found fused with a predominance of native beliefs and practices in many of these, and only the Feast of All Souls, Yü-lan-p'en-hui (Sanskrit Avalambana), is unmistakably Buddhist. Even in this

---

[16] Francis L. K. Hsu, *Under the Ancestors' Shadow* (New York, 1948), p. 173.

observance elements of other cults—particularly the family cult—are introduced, and the use of basins (*p'en*) for making offerings is derived from the misapprehension that the character *p'en*, "basin," which was simply a transliteration of the Sanskrit syllable *ban*, enjoined the use of basins in the festival.[17]

Even as the pantheons and cults of Buddhism and religious Taoism tended to fuse, so did the roles and functions of their clergies. Modern observers have found Taoist adepts in charge of nominally Buddhist shrines and Buddhist monks officiating in Taoist temples. Functionally the two clergies tended to merge; both served as exorcists and healers, both were called upon to pray for rain, and both might be called in for funeral services. Shrines of the tutelary divinities of villages or towns, whose origins go back to remote antiquity, might have either a Buddhist or a Taoist cleric in charge. The two clergies also shared the contumely of the literati, who, unlike their predecessors in the T'ang, could glory in a self-sufficient thought system, albeit one that had initially drawn much of its intellectual sustenance from Buddhism and Taoism.

The process of appropriation which we have considered at the elite and peasant levels of society is also to be observed in developments which are not strictly associated with either of these strata. For example, the clan organizations which are a feature of Chinese society from the Sung onward cut across class lines and bound broad kinship groups together in mutual enterprises and common ceremonial ob-

---

[17] Cf. Derk Bodde, trans., *Annual Customs and Festivals in Peking* (Peking, 1936), p. 62.

servances. Certain features of these organizations, notably the idea and function of charitable estates for the benefit of the whole clan, are of Buddhist origin.[18] Buddhist elements were occasionally incorporated into the codes which governed clan life, yet the basis of these codes was the neo-Confucian lay ethic, and the ideas of karma and retribution were introduced merely as ancillary sanctions to restrain the evildoer.[19]

Again, Buddhist symbolism, mingled with elements from Confucianism and popular Taoism, is to be seen in the ideologies and rituals of the secret societies which figured so largely in Chinese life from the twelfth or thirteenth century onward. Witness the frequent recurrence of the term for "white"—the symbolic color of the Maitreya cult—in the names of such societies as the Pai lien chiao (White Lotus Society) and Pai yün hui (White Cloud Society). But if some of these societies claimed a dubious descent from Buddhist devotional organizations of an earlier day, they became, in modern times, little more than pseudo-kinship groups held together by the interests—occult, economic, social, and political—of their membership. The functions filled by family-supported Buddhist temples and by religious organizations in the days of Buddhist dominance were now taken over by the clans and the secret societies, and Buddhist elements were selectively appropriated whenever they seemed useful.

---

[18] See Denis Twitchett, "The Fan Clan's Charitable Estates, 1050–1760." To appear in *Confucianism in Action* (Stanford, 1959).

[19] Cf. Hui-chen Wang Liu, "An Analysis of the Clan Rules." To appear in *Confucianism in Action* (Stanford, 1959).

The concept of karma, in its Sinicized form, is to be found in all types of literature, from the poetry of the elite to the tales of the popular storytellers. In stories and drama it provides a ready plotting device and an explanation of untoward events, of the virtuous being unrewarded and the vicious flourishing like the green bay tree. In the everyday thought of all classes it formed part of a common explanation of reward and retribution which, in its essentials, goes back to pre-Buddhist times. Before Buddhism divine retribution was believed to fall upon families; Buddhism then introduced the idea of karmic causation, but this was on an individual basis. Finally the two were interwoven into the view that has prevailed since the Sung period; that divine retribution works on a family basis *and* through a chain of lives.[20]

The process of appropriation may be further observed in a variety of common objects and their decoration. Cammann has shown how elements of Buddhist iconography were taken into the secular arts, where they were gradually deformed and eventually degenerated into meaningless ornamentation.[21] A close examination of almost any piece of recent cloisonné or porcelain will reveal the Buddhist origin of many of its routinized decorative motifs.

These must suffice to illustrate the varieties of appropriation characteristic of the long period from the tenth century to the nineteenth. The process of appropriation as we have

---

[20] Cf. Lien-sheng Yang, "The Concept of *Pao* as a Basis for Social Relations in China," in J. K. Fairbank, ed., *Chinese Thought and Institutions* (Chicago, 1957), pp. 291–309.

[21] Schuyler Cammann, "Types of Symbols in Chinese Art," in Arthur F. Wright, ed., *Studies in Chinese Thought* (Chicago, 1953), pp. 211–14.

observed it calls attention to some of the limitations and vul-
nerabilities of Buddhism as a religion. Toynbee has observed that the Mahayana is a politically incompetent religion, and we should say that its record in China bears this
out.[22] Despite its occasional use for political purposes—e.g.,
to sanctify power and to justify war—it was prevented by its
basic postulate of the delusive and transitory character of
earthly existence from developing a comprehensive political
theory. Its adherents, for the most part, were resigned to
any regime which might, for good or ill, control some por-
tion of a universe of illusion for what was only a split second
in infinite time. Buddhist monks sometimes acted for political ends, but they were constrained by their own outlook and
their own discipline (the Vinaya) as well as by measures of
governmental control, and were thus prevented from building a "church" which could achieve the socio-political dominance that Christianity once had in the Western world.

The educated Buddhist clergy tended to become more
and more withdrawn from the laity and to cede the sphere
of political and social action as well as the realm of the arts
to the neo-Confucians. The rural clergy tended, as we have
seen, to become little more than priests of an undifferentiated
folk religion, serving local peasant needs without demanding
adherence to any creed or regimen. There was neither a
militant, indoctrinated clergy nor an organized, disciplined
laity. Thus neo-Confucianism formed and dominated the
Apollonian culture of the elite, while ancient folk beliefs and
mores—influenced, but not dominated, by neo-Confucian-

---

[22] Arnold Toynbee, *A Study of History*, IX (London, 1954), 40–41.

ism—reasserted control over the Dionysiac culture of the masses.

Buddhism nonetheless contributed much to both the elite and popular cultures of modern China. As we have seen, the appropriation of Buddhism was not a process of "absorption" in the sense of swallowing up, assimilation without a trace. Appropriation never is. That "China absorbs its ethnic and cultural invaders" is a hoary and delusive myth, and its falsity is nowhere better demonstrated than in the process just reviewed.

Our consideration of the appropriation of Buddhism at the elite and popular levels brings us to the eve of the break-up of imperial China. In the next chapter we shall deal with the role and significance of Chinese Buddhism in the twentieth century. There we shall speculate on the meaning of the long history we have reviewed and on Buddhism's possible contributions to the Chinese culture of tomorrow.

CHAPTER SIX

THE LEGACY OF BUDDHISM IN CHINA

In examining the legacy of Buddhism in modern China, it is useful to consider two levels. One comprises the elements of thought, language, and culture which have been so completely appropriated that their provenance is forgotten. The other consists of self-conscious efforts to identify, reinterpret, and use elements of the Buddhist heritage to meet the problems of a China whose traditional civilization crumbled under the impact of forces generated in the modern West. In examining the Buddhist legacy at these two levels, we shall again be concerned with the differences between elite and popular cultures, with those contrasting attitudes and interests that have figured so largely in the whole historic process of the interaction of Buddhism and Chinese culture.

One of the most palpable and pervasive legacies of Buddhism is to be found in the Chinese language of modern times. From the proverbs of the peasant villages to the formal language of the intelligentsia, words of Buddhist origin are found in common use by people who are quite unconscious of their origin. For example, the common name for glass (*po-li*) is a corruption of a transliterated Sanskrit word, and the names of many precious and semi-precious stones are of similar origin; so are the terms for many trees and plants. Other words for common objects, gestures, and expressions are used with a special meaning originally given them in Buddhist usage. Still others, coined for Buddhist purposes, entered the secular vocabulary with quite a different meaning.[1]

Buddhism left still another linguistic legacy. When Western culture invaded China in the nineteenth and twentieth centuries and the missionaries of religion, of Western technology, and of political ideologies introduced into China for the second time in its history a wide range of foreign ideas and foreign terminology, the new challenge was met largely with the help of resources developed in the centuries of effort to deal with Indian languages: improved techniques of phonological and grammatical analysis,[2] and, of more immediate and general utility, the stock of linguistic devices developed and conventionalized for expressing Indian words and ideas. Once again the invading culture expressed its ideas in inflected polysyllables, and the characters invented for the transliteration of Indian and Central Asian words were now put to new uses. Proper names from the Bible and from Western history and philosophy, untranslatable terms from the sciences and the humanities, were now introduced into Chinese by means of transliterative devices originally developed to render the untranslatable words of Indian origin. These devices now served to intro-

---

[1] Cf. Thomas Watters, *Essays on the Chinese Language* (Shanghai, 1889), pp. 379–496.

[2] Cf. A. von Rosthorn, "Indischer Einfluss in der Lautlehre Chinas," *Sitzungsberichte, Akademie der Wissenschaften in Wien,* CCXIX (1941), p. 22.

duce innumerable Western ideas; for example, "romantic," which had no Chinese analogue, became *lang-manti*, "modern" became *mo-teng*, "motor" became *mo-t'o*. Few, if any, of the missionaries of Western culture or the Chinese translators were fully aware of the rich store of relevant experience available to them in the records of Buddhist translators who had grappled with similar problems a millennium and a half earlier, but the modern interpreter of things Western was, however unconsciously, greatly in their debt.

In Chapter Five we noted many elements of the cultural legacy of Buddhism in China. Here we might mention the popular notions of karma and the after-life, the gods of folk religion, festivals whose symbols and observances suggest their Buddhist origin, decorative motifs in architecture and the lesser arts, and literary and musical genres and conventions which in times past were enriched by borrowings from Buddhism. We might extend this list almost indefinitely, but it is plain that Buddhism had ceased to be a definable tradition, a coherent body of belief, or a distinct way of life. The tradition had become fragmented, and elements introduced during the long period we have considered had fused with one or another strand of indigenous culture. Not until the new pressures of the late nineteenth and early twentieth centuries made themselves felt did a few Chinese seek to revive and reconstruct Chinese Buddhism as a separate and integral tradition. A brief consideration of these efforts may perhaps shed light on the whole historical process we have been reviewing.

The background of the modern rediscovery of Chinese Buddhism is of course the erosion and break-up of Chinese civilization itself. During the hundred years of ever-deepening crisis after 1850, the intelligentsia—the Confucian literati—were first the self-conscious defenders of their civilization, then its critics and reformers. Finally, when nothing but the rubble of traditional civilization remained, these men led the quest for new ideas and institutions which, they hoped, might provide the basis for a new and viable Chinese order. One of many critical observations of Chinese society in its modern crisis was that the literati, with their once self-sufficient neo-Confucian way and view of life, were separated by a wide gulf from the peasant masses, to which the old order permitted a Buddho-Taoist religion of many gods and many cults. Modern Chinese observers of the deepening crisis in their society looked for a solution toward the modern West, where they thought they saw nations socially united and invigorated by a common faith. For the great reformer K'ang Yu-wei (1858–1927), who had devoted himself for a time to Buddhist studies, the remedy lay in a remodeled Confucianism that could serve as the religion of a modernized state. Others turned to the heritage of Chinese Buddhism.

As the pace of social and political disintegration increased, Chinese intellectuals were driven to a cultural defensiveness which set them to ransacking their own history for analogues or prefigurings of the Western ideas whose truth seemed unanswerable in the light of their world-wide success in action. This kind of cultural defensiveness spread over most of Asia, and in China and elsewhere it often centered some of its defenses in the Buddhist tradition. Paul Demiéville sums it up:

They endeavor first of all to show that the Occident has invented nothing and that Buddhism, for example, is democratic, since it is essentially egalitarian and the decisions of the monastic communities were reached by majority vote; that it is humanistic, since man alone counts in the canonical doctrine; that it is communistic, since the primitive religious community was classless and its property collectively owned; that it is rationalist, since salvation is a matter of reason divorced from all transcendence; that in its doctrine of the Void and its dialectic it is Kantian and Hegelian; that it is existentialist in its denial of all essence and its insistence on suffering; that it is, in the theories of the School of Knowledge, the precursor of Freud and Jung. Certain of these diverse traits (they admit) are not always present in Buddhism as it exists, but one need only reform it to adapt it to the modern world and put it in a condition to stand up to Christianity or even to Marxism.[3]

The writings of the reformer Liang Ch'i-ch'ao express this cultural defensiveness, and when he speaks of Buddhism, it is to claim the superiority of the doctrine of Karma over the theories of Darwin and Spencer, to point to the more advanced form of Western libertarianism to be found in Buddhism, and so on. Moreover, he claims for China the key role in the formation of the Mahayana, and thus adds to the list of Chinese priorities and superiorities with which he seeks to revive his own and his countrymen's waning confidence in the creativity of their culture.[4]

---

[3] Paul Demiéville, "Les Religions de l'Orient et de l'extrême-Orient: Tendances actuelles," *Encyclopédie française*, XIX (Paris, 1957), 54/1.

[4] Cf. J. R. Levenson, *Liang Ch'i-ch'ao and the Mind of Modern China* (Cambridge, Mass., 1953), pp. 129–32.

Still another and quite different stimulus to the re-examination of China's Buddhist heritage arose from a general reappraisal of Chinese history, often guided by the consciously or unconsciously posed question: "What has brought our civilization from the heights of greatness to the depths of chaos and humiliation?" Hu Shih and other scholars began the great task of rediscovering those Buddhist chapters of Chinese history that Confucian historians had largely ignored. Hu Shih's ultimate findings amounted to an indictment of Buddhism. He found that it was Buddhism that had deflected the humane, rational, and proto-scientific culture of China from an orderly course of development which would have made Chinese civilization fully the equal of the West's in the modern world. He points to the failure of the neo-Confucians "to revive a secular thought and to build up a secular society to take the place of the other-worldly religions of Medieval China. They failed because they were powerless against the dead weight of over a thousand years of Indianization." And his prescription for Chinese backwardness follows naturally from this: "With the new aids of modern science and technology, and of the new social and historical sciences, we are confident that we may yet achieve a rapid liberation from the two thousand years' cultural domination by India."[5]

In addition to these seekers after a new social cement, or cultural parity with the West, or an explanation of the lack of such parity, there were those who looked to a modernized

---

[5] Cf. Hu Shih, "The Indianization of China: A Case Study in Cultural Borrowing," in *Independence, Convergence and Borrowing,* Harvard Tercentenary Publications (Cambridge, Mass., 1937), p. 247.

Buddhism as a new ideology for an Eastern Asia united in a common stand against the intruding West. The Japanese empire-builders and their Chinese collaborators in the years 1937 to 1945 rebuilt and repaired temples, sponsored societies of lay Buddhists, and attempted to use Sino-Japanese Buddhism as a bond between the two peoples in what was represented as their common struggle against Western imperialism. This effort failed, but the attempt to make tactical use of Buddhism in the international politics of Eastern Asia is now continued by the People's Government in Peking. The preface to a recent Chinese Communist volume on Buddhism states this aim clearly: "Chinese Buddhists have united with the people of the whole country to give active support to China's socialist construction and to protect world peace. . . . To propagate Buddha's holy teachings and to safeguard world peace, Chinese Buddhists are eager to strengthen their friendship and co-operation with the Buddhists of other countries."[6]

These varieties of revived interest in Buddhism manifested themselves in a wide range of intellectual, political, and social activities. If we consider a few of these, we may be led to general reflections on some persisting disabilities which Buddhism labored under in modern China and on its possible role in a future Chinese culture.

It is significant that most of the serious revival of Buddhism in modern China was the work of laymen—people who felt that Buddhist ethics might reunite a divided society and Buddhist thought deepen men's awareness of the changing world in which they lived. The lay leaders ob-

---

[6] Cf. *Buddhists in New China* (Peking, 1956), p. 5.

served that the older Buddhist clergy, if educated, were sunk in lethargy and despair—their defeatism rationalized by the doctrine that one who lived in a period of "the extinction of the dharma" (*mo-fa*) could do little but look to his own salvation. The lay Buddhists organized themselves in a variety of efforts to revitalize and update Buddhism for modern China. Publishing houses were started, magazines and books were published, the sacred texts were reedited and reprinted. Although study groups and devotional groups were founded in many provinces, the center of the new activity was in the Yangtze valley and in the southern coastal provinces. There were national conferences on religious and social problems, fund-raising drives for new seminaries to train a modern clergy, efforts to establish modern organizations such as the YMBA and the YWBA. In 1914 the Chinese Buddhist Association was founded to fight the effort to make Confucianism a state religion. It continued as a nation-wide organization of laity and clergy to defend and promote Buddhist interests. Yet for fairly obvious reasons its structure was loose and ineffectual, and no great leaders emerged to give it vitality.

All the new activities were confined for the most part to the educated class, and Buddhism remained socially stratified; for the literate there were refurbished Buddhist ideas and a scattering of modernized institutions; the peasantry were left with their old Sinicized cults and a corrupt and illiterate Buddho-Taoist clergy. We noted that the social stratification of religion began to have serious effects on Buddhism after the decline of the T'ang order. The Buddhist revival in modern China failed to bridge that chasm.

We may say that this was a failure of drive, of vision, of vitality, but we shall have to seek a fuller explanation in the doctrinal and institutional limitations which Buddhism inherited from its past.

The intellectual appeal of Buddhism in modern China has not been sufficient to attract more than a handful of the new political and social leaders. Many of these leaders received their education in the last days of the old order, and they were indoctrinated with neo-Confucianism's dislike and disdain for Buddhist thought. The ideas and technical terms were difficult yet lacking in the novelty and the aura of success which accompanied the new ideas from the West. Buddhism—for all its new social consciousness—seemed to many to teach a lesson of passivity or tolerant resignation at a time when the mood of the intellectuals and political leaders called for a program of positive action. This revulsion against the passivity of Sino-Indian religion was well expressed by Ch'en Tu-hsiu, later to become one of the founders of the Chinese Communist party. He maintained that whereas the West had won its preeminence through strenuous conflict and blood, the East was inert, pacificistic, and helpless. He espoused Western militancy and dynamism: "The Oriental peoples may regard all this as madness, but in what condition do all these Oriental people, with their love of peace, quiet and harmony, now find themselves?"[7] That Ch'en and men like him trafficked in dubious clichés should not obscure the fact that they were passionately seek-

    [7] Cf. Benjamin I. Schwartz, "Ch'en Tu-hsiu and the Acceptance of the Modern West," in Arthur F. Wright, ed., "Chinese Reactions to Imported Ideas," *Journal of the History of Ideas,* XII (1951), 65.

ing a solution for China's ills, and that the Buddhist ethos as they understood it was anathema to them.

Another disability of Buddhism and one that made its revival in modern China abortive was its apolitical character. We have noted its political passivity, its subservience to the state, throughout most of its history in China, and this appeared anachronistic to modern Chinese who had their eyes on the independent and militant religions of the West. Buddhist clergy and laymen made their peace with the warlords of North China, with the Japanese puppet regimes of the period of the Sino-Japanese War, and with a Kuomintang which had taken the most draconian measures against temples and clergy; this passivity was damning in the eyes of those who favored revolutionary change or a pluralistic society with a new balance of power between the state and groups united by common beliefs.

For centuries Buddhist apologists had sought to delineate the spheres of Buddhist and of Confucian doctrines and beliefs by saying that whereas Confucianism prescribed in detail for the here-and-now, Buddhism overarched it at both ends by interpreting the past, the present, and the future in a single continuum. Yet this continuum was a spiritual one, an explanation of the individual's destiny in terms of his past deeds, present acts, and future reward or retribution. In modern China two burning interests worked to exclude Buddhism from the spectrum of intellectual choice. One was precisely the overriding concern with the here-and-now, with the diagnosis of China's desperate illness and prescriptions for its cure. The other was linked to this; it was a concern for the collectivity that was China, whether regarded as nation, society, or civilization. These two concerns tended to focus intellectual interest, not on the spiritual destiny of the individual, but on theories of history and society which claimed to explain the dynamics of states, of economies, and of societies. Buddhism had no such theory to offer, and it lost by default to the rising tide of evolutionary and materialist doctrines which seemed to offer the Chinese both an explanation of their plight and formulas which would put China on one or another allegedly universal escalator of progress.

Around the great and pressing problems of China's plight and its possible future a fierce controversy raged. One phase of this controversy was the debate on "Science and Philosophy of Life" in 1923, in which the real issue was not whether science was or was not superior to metaphysical thought, but *which* outlook would help China regain its strength, integrity, and self-respect. Those who continued to speak in religious or metaphysical terms, whether European or Asian, came in for a variety of attacks. Those who followed Russell, Dewey, and, in increasing numbers, Marx, asserted that the "age of religion" was a thing of the past in all advanced countries and that China in its march to modernity should take no backward steps.

This view was given wide public expression in the anti-religious movement of the 1920's; among other things, the cry went up that the West was seeking, through its missionaries, to saddle China with the incubus of religion which the West itself had finally succeeded in throwing off. The right to spread Christianity was included in the unequal treaties that were deeply resented and incessantly denounced by all parties and groups. Nor was it forgotten that the right to send Buddhist missionaries had been exacted by Japan in the treaties she imposed on a prostrate China. When Tagore visited China in 1924 and preached the doctrine of the superiority of Eastern spirituality over Western materialism, he was attacked as a living symbol of the futile passivity of Eastern religions, a passivity that had reduced India to colonial and China to semi-colonial status. His appeal to open up the overgrown paths of cultural contact between India and China and unite the countries in a common spirituality fell on deaf ears.[8] Neither his message nor the manifestoes of modernizing Buddhists offered any concrete and comprehensive formula for the salvation of China.

As we have seen, Buddhism was used by Chinese governments as an instrument of foreign policy from the Sui and T'ang, through the Manchu dynasty's use of Lamaism, down to Mao Tse-tung's tactical use of Buddhism in his relations with the rest of Asia. But there were also Chinese who sincerely regarded Buddhism as a supra-national faith that might unite the peoples of Eastern Asia in common resistance to the West and in the solution of their common problems. Tagore's spiritual pan-Asianism was rejected, but Chinese Buddhist groups made continuing efforts to establish their own Chinese variety of Buddhist internationalism. Yet when they asserted the international character of Buddhism they encountered two forms of resistance, both formidable. One was a pervasive xenophobia, a product of foreign pressure and Chinese frustration during nearly a century of crisis. The other was the rising tide of nationalist fervor,

---

[8] Cf. Stephen N. Hay, "India's Prophet in East Asia: Tagore's Message of Pan-Asian Spiritual Revival and Its Reception in Japan and China, 1916–1929," Ph.D. thesis, Harvard, 1957.

particularly after 1919, that rallied Chinese in increasing numbers to what was exclusively and distinctively their own. Internationalism—Buddhist, Christian, or any other variety —was in conflict with a nationalism that for decades was the only article of faith on which all Chinese could agree. When Japan, in its own imperial interests, sponsored a Buddhist internationalism designed to smooth the path to conquest and foster docility and acceptance among the conquered, Buddhism became detestable in the eyes of patriotic and nationalistic Chinese. Not only did they resent this use of Buddhism as an instrument of psychological warfare, they also noted the subservience of Japan's "modernized" Buddhist clergy to the will of a tyrannical and aggressive state; and from this they drew the lesson—justifiably or not is hardly the issue—that a modernized Chinese Buddhist clergy might well become the instrument of tyranny and reaction in their own country.

The invasion of China by the secular faiths of the modern West placed Buddhism in an arena of competition for which its history had ill prepared it. Faith in science was propagated by Dewey and Russell. The great abbot T'ai-hsü (1889–1946), the leading spokesman for a modernized Buddhism, might reply to the missionaries of science that Buddhism had long ago discovered the atom and relativity, that its psychological science was far more advanced than that of the West, but his critics would retort in effect: "What did you do with your discoveries? Did they liberate men's minds and contribute to a freer and a more abundant life, or did they remain the intellectual playthings of monastic speculation?" To reply was difficult, for Buddhism had in fact emphasized the apprehension of reality and faith in Buddhas and Bodhisattvas as means to release from an ephemeral and illusory world. Its effects on society had been the by-products of the spread of a faith and not of a concerted or planned effort to build a new society on the basis of Buddhist ideas.

The rising tide of materialist thought in this century saw the steady ebb of interest in idealisms, whether Chinese, Western, or Indian. It was against this intellectual background that the secular faith of Marxism steadily gained ground until it was finally imposed upon all Chinese by a militant minority.

Since 1949 Buddhism has suffered the fate of other organized religions in China. Its struggling schools and publishing houses have been taken over; its temples and clergy have been secularized on a large scale; stripped of their long-dwindling property, the few remaining temples and their monks exist at the pleasure of the government. The modern nation-wide organization of Chinese Buddhists, originally set up for the defense and propagation of the faith, has been revived as part of the complex network of organizations through which the government controls the people of China. The great monuments of Chinese Buddhism are being systematically restored not as centers of worship but as shrines to the "cultural creativity of the Chinese people under the feudal empires of the past."

In the course of this revolutionary process, Buddhism has once again adapted itself to political change. Though many suffered and died, few martyrs and no new martyrology have emerged from the recent period of strife. The secular faith of Marxism-Leninism has been made the center of all thought and value, and adherence to it is the only path to worldly success. Officially approved Buddhist apologists strain to prove—and not for the first time in Chinese history—that Buddhism is wholly compatible with a creed ordained by the state. Elderly Buddhists meet for prayers and sutra readings under portraits of Chairman Mao, and the residue of organized Buddhism is barely tolerated as an adjunct of Communist minority and foreign policies.

We are seeing, I believe, the last twilight of Chinese Buddhism as an organized religion. The dispersed fragments of its cults and beliefs are being systematically extirpated throughout the whole of society. The Communist war on "superstition" in the villages is unremitting, and one wonders how long the peasantry will cling to its Buddho-Taoist folk religion. The secret societies, with ideologies drawn from Buddhist, Taoist, and Confucian sources, have been ruthlessly suppressed along with every other form of association that challenges the monopoly by the state and the party of all matters of belief and behavior.

If, in the years to come, we look for the legacy of Buddhism in China, we shall perhaps find it still in literature and language, in drama and the arts. And if we watch closely the steps by which the Chinese seek to build a new composite culture out of selected elements from their own traditions blended with Western borrowings, we shall note the long-term effect of the Buddhist experience. Typically it will appear as it does in statements like that of Liu Shao-ch'i—the leading theoretician of Chinese Communism—when he says that the ideal Communist party member "grieves before all the rest of the world grieves and is happy only after all the rest of the world is happy." Here is a restatement of Fan Chung-yen's ideal of the Confucian scholar, an ideal appropriated from Buddhism nearly a millennium ago.[9] It would seem that so long as there are Chinese speaking the Chinese language and dealing with their problems in ways that are distinctively the product of their common heritage, an awareness of the legacy of Buddhism will help us to understand their thought and behavior.

*   *   *

As we look back over the two thousand years of history surveyed in these pages, there seem to be certain general observations that we can make about the characteristics of Chinese civilization, and about certain of its persistent and recurrent patterns.

First, we should observe that one persisting ideal of the Chinese is the notion of their culture as a whole self-consistent entity. History records much that is at odds with this, as with all ideals. Yet we find the Chinese returning again and again to the ideal of a monolithic society, economy, and polity, supported and rationalized by a thought system that is wholly consistent with itself and with the institutions it supports. The Han order approximated this ideal, and in the Sui and the T'ang, Buddhism was more or less successfully integrated into the effort to recapture the Han ideal. Later, however, when circumstances had changed, the Sung synthesis rejected any separate and distinctive Buddhism as in conflict with the ancient holistic ideal of Chinese civiliza-

---

[9] Liu Shao-ch'i, *Lun kung-ch'ang-tang-yüan ti hsiu-yang* (Hongkong ed. of 1949), pp. 30–32. Discussed by David S. Nivison in "Communist Ethics and Chinese Tradition," *Journal of Asian Studies*, XVI (1956), 60.

tion, and appropriated only such parts of the faith as were compatible with this ideal. Most recently we have seen a new reintegration that is more complete, more totalitarian in its broadest sense, than anything in China's previous history. Once again an orthodoxy imposed by the state supports and rationalizes an institutional order allegedly consistent with the approved system of ideas. To the degree that this ideal is realized, all competing ideas, religious or secular, are rejected or suppressed.

Second, we might observe that periods of disintegration and the loss of the holistic and related ideals are the only periods in which Chinese have shown any responsiveness to alien ideas. Buddhism could no more have established itself in the Empire of Han than Catholic Christianity could in the prosperous years of the Ch'ing dynasty. There are many similarities between the period of disunion from about 300 to 589 and the nineteenth and twentieth centuries. In the first, an age of chaos and experimentation, the foreign ideas of Buddhism were the object of interest and commitment. In the second, first Christianity and then the secular faiths of the West have attracted those who sought a solution to the crisis of their civilization. In both these periods one sees an iconoclastic attitude toward ancient traditions, a restless, often passionate search for something new. In the ages that followed the first period we observed the reworking, then the appropriation, of what had been taken from an alien religion. On what will follow the present age we can only speculate, remembering that the erosion of native traditions has now gone much further than ever before. What we have seen of the role of Buddhism in the development of Chinese civilization may help us to understand the process of borrowing and adaptation that is now going on and to analyze whatever cultural synthesis may emerge in the future.

Third, we should do well to note the fatuity of the notion of "absorption" as an explanation of what China does with elements of alien cultures. Just as innumerable invasions of alien people have not left the Chinese physical type unchanged, so what came in with Buddhism was not simply absorbed; it was appropriated and became part of a new cultural synthesis utterly different from that which had preceded this experience. The image of China as the sea that salts all the streams which flow into it does violence to the history of Buddhism in China, and it will mislead those who invoke it as a clue to the future of Chinese culture.

Fourth, the history of Buddhism in China demonstrates, as the history of Communism has more recently done, the Chinese capacity for fanatical commitment to an idea or a way of life. The West, in its appraisal of Chinese culture, has been the victim of the self-image of the civilization—the myth that was the property of the neo-Confucian elite of recent times. One element of that self-image was that the Chinese were consistently ethnocentric, rational, and humanistic. The Jesuits were taken in by this myth and propagated it in the West, where it lingers today. We have noted the fanatical commitment which characterized the Yellow Turban movement, and we have pointed to the wave of religious enthusiasm, the passionate acts of sacrifice and renunciation, which characterized the high tide of Buddhism in China.

If you wish evidence of the persistence of this capacity in the present, I commend to you the chapter entitled "The Red Nun" in Father Green's *Calvary in China*.[10]

Fifth, we have often noted in these pages the degree of authority which the Chinese state perennially claimed over matters of behavior and belief. Sometimes the state was unable to assert this control, but its right to do so was never renounced. In the long history of Buddhism we saw state power used to modify and to restrict both thought and action; we also observed the pragmatic and utilitarian use of selected religious beliefs that the state could not extirpate but chose to use for social control. Much of the failure of the Buddhist church to preserve its doctrinal integrity can be traced to this implacable state pressure and state policy. In modern China the same tendency is to be observed. The Communist regime does not choose at this time to extirpate Christianity, Islam, or Buddhism; from the point of view of international politics this would not be expedient. But the Communist state *uses* selected religious doctrines whenever and wherever these serve its tactical purposes. The tragic apologists of the three faiths acknowledge this time-honored power of Chinese governments and cooperate in emphasizing those beliefs that the state has decided are useful for the moment.

I should like to stress that I do not believe that history ever repeats itself in such a way as to provide a basis for prediction. The people who say that the regime of Mao Tse-tung is "just another dynasty" are quite as mistaken as those who say that China's break with its past is sharp and

---

[10] Robert W. Green, M.M., *Calvary in China* (New York, 1953), pp. 61–73.

complete. The great formative experiences of a people's collective past seem to me, if they are rightly understood, to explain what that civilization has become in our time and to suggest some of the ways in which it will respond to the challenges it faces now and those it will face in the future. One of the formative experiences of the Chinese people was their age-long effort to deal with the religion and culture that came to them from India. To the degree that we ignore or misinterpret the history of that experience, we shall go astray in our efforts to understand the life, the culture, and the character of a great people.

A SELECTION OF FURTHER READINGS

This selection is limited to books and articles in Western languages that are reasonably accessible. The writings of modern Chinese and Japanese scholars available in translation are a small and unrepresentative sample of the wealth of creative scholarship in those languages—scholarship that has revolutionized the study of Chinese Buddhism in our time. The reader who may wish to pursue a particular interest or survey the range of modern studies of Buddhism should consult the annual publication *Bibliographie bouddhique* (32 fascicules, Paris, 1930–67); it contains full notices of important works in all languages and valuable retrospective accounts of the writings of distinguished scholars. For ready reference one may consult the section devoted to Buddhism in Charles Adams, ed., *A Reader's Guide to the Great Religions* (Chicago, 1965).

GENERAL STUDIES

Despite the steady accumulation of excellent specialized works, the reader will look in vain for a survey which sums up all earlier studies of Buddhism as Sir Charles Eliot did in his *Hinduism and Buddhism* (3 vols., London, 1921). Much of this is now long out of date. Perhaps the best historical account of the evolution of religious doctrine and practice is still E. J. Thomas, *The History of Buddhist Thought* (London, 1933; 2d ed., 1951). By far the most important synoptic work on Chinese

Buddhism is Kenneth Ch'en, *Buddhism in China, A Historical Survey* (Princeton, 1964). A recent and readable collection of papers on the Buddhisms of southern and eastern Asia is *The Path of the Buddha*, edited by Kenneth W. Morgan (New York, 1956). Although some chapters are more informed by piety than critical scholarship, the historical essay on Buddhism in China and Korea by Zenryū Tsukamoto presents an interpretation by the most distinguished Japanese scholar in this field. A survey of doctrinal development is Edward Conze's admirable volume *Buddhism, Its Essence and Development* (London and New York, 1951).

For the philosophic ideas of the Mahayana as they were interpreted in China and Japan, the patient reader will find useful insights in the late Junjiro Takakusu's *The Essentials of Buddhist Philosophy* (Honolulu, 1947). In contrast to Takakusu's approach to Buddhist ideas as the unfolding of divine truths, Professor Paul Demiéville has analyzed some of these concepts with the methods of a historian of ideas. His article "La Pénétration du Bouddhisme dans la tradition philosophique chinoise," *Journal of World History*, III (1956), is a brilliant interpretation by a master of this field of study. The second volume of Fung Yu-lan's *History of Chinese Philosophy*, as translated by Derk Bodde (Princeton, 1953), deals at length with Chinese Buddhist philosophers, but the author's Confucian bias is somewhat obtrusive.

In the field of cultural history, *India and China: A Thousand Years of Cultural Relations* (Bombay, 2d ed., 1950) by the late Prabodh Chandra Bagchi is interesting and readable. The author brought an Indian viewpoint to this study, along with a wide knowledge of Chinese Buddhist history and its sources. A contrasting picture of Sino-Indian cultural relations stressing the negative effects on Chinese culture is to be found in Dr.

Hu Shih's essay "The Indianization of China" in the Harvard Tercentenary publication *Independence, Convergence and Borrowing in Institutions, Thought and Art* (Cambridge, Mass., 1937). If the reader prefers to approach the history of Chinese Buddhism in relation to the history of Chinese religion as a whole, the writings of the late Henri Maspero are unexcelled. See, for example, his essay "La Religion chinoise dans son developpement historique" in his *Mélanges posthumes sur les religions et l'histoire de la Chine*, Vol. I (Paris, 1950).

For a survey of the complex history of Buddhist scriptures in China and of their translation and interpretation, one should consult Bagchi's study *Le Canon bouddhique en Chine* (2 vols.; Paris, 1926, 1938).

HISTORICAL STUDIES AND BIOGRAPHIES

On the breakup of the Han order and its aftermath, two studies by Etienne Balazs, now translated from the French, are of prime importance: "Political Philosophy and Social Crisis at the End of the Han Dynasty" and "Nihilistic Revolt or Mystical Escapism: Currents of Thought in China During the Third Century A.D." They appear in the collection of his essays entitled *Chinese Civilization and Bureaucracy: Variations on a Theme* (New Haven, 1964). Henri Maspero's popular account of his scholarly studies on the introduction of Buddhism is enlightening. It is entitled "Comment le Bouddhisme s'est introduit en Chine" and appears in Vol. I of his *Mélanges posthumes*.

Writings on the development of Buddhism in the period of disunion are scattered and few. Kenneth Ch'en's paper on anti-Buddhist measures of the northern dynasties appeared in *Harvard Journal of Asiatic Studies*, XVII (1954), and his companion study on anti-Buddhism in the south in Vol. XV of the same journal (1952). My study of the pioneer missionary Fo-t'u-teng is to be found in the same journal, Vol. XI (1948), and Arthur Link's annotated biography of Fo-t'u-teng's leading disciple appears in T'oung Pao, XLVI (1958). Recently Robert Shih has begun to publish translations from the mid-sixth-century collection of monks' biographies, the *Kao-seng Chuan* of Hui-chiao. The first installment, the lives of the early translators, has appeared under the title *Biographies des Moines éminents* (Louvain, 1968). Perhaps the most detailed study of a leading southern monk of the period of disunion is to be found in the series of articles by Walter Liebenthal on Chu Tao-sheng which appeared in *Monumenta Nipponica*, XI–XII (Tokyo, 1955–57). The best available translation of the official historical account of Buddhism in this period is by Zenryū Tsukamoto as translated by Leon Hurvitz. This appears as a supplement to Volume XVI of the magnificent series on the cave-temples of Yün-kang by Seiichi Mizuno and Toshio Nagahiro (Kyoto, 1956). James Legge's translation of the account of a Buddhist pilgrimage to India between 399 and 414, *The Travels of Fa-Hien* (Oxford, 1886), may still be read with profit.

The history of the Chinese Buddhist sects of the Sui and T'ang has been little studied. On the school of meditation one may still consult Hu Shih, "The Development of Zen Buddhism in China," *The Chinese Social and Political Science Review*, XV (Peking, 1932), reprinted in *Sino-Indian Studies*, III (Santiniketan, 1949). *The Development of Chinese Zen* by Heinrich Dumoulin, S.J., and Ruth Fuller Sasaki (New York, 1953) may well seem over-technical to the general reader. Leon Hurvitz has published a major study of the founder of the T'ien-t'ai school entitled *Chih-I (538–597), An Introduction to the Life and Ideas of a Chinese Buddhist Monk*, Vol. XII of the *Mélanges chinois et bouddhiques* (Bruges, 1963). Chou Yi-liang's "Tantrism in China," *Harvard Journal of Asiatic*

Studies, VIII (1945), studies the history of the introduction of this late Mahayana school in T'ang times.

The relation between Buddhism and the state in this period is discussed in my study of a noted anti-Buddhist whose life spanned the end of the period of disunion, the Sui, and the early T'ang: "Fu I and the Rejection of Buddhism," *Journal of the History of Ideas*, XII (1951). On the ideological uses of Buddhism by the Sui, see my article "The Formation of Sui Ideology," in John K. Fairbank, ed., *Chinese Thought and Institutions* (Chicago, 1957). An important paper by Stanley Weinstein entitled "Imperial Patronage in the Formation of T'ang Buddhism" will appear in A. F. Wright and D. C. Twitchett, eds., *Perspectives on the T'ang* (New Haven, 1973); the same volume contains my study "T'ai-tsung and Buddhism." The most vivid and readable account of Buddhism in T'ang life and culture is Edwin Reischauer's excellent volume *Ennin's Travels in T'ang China* (New York, 1955). The companion volume, *Ennin's Diary* (New York, 1955), is a translation of the day-by-day account of an assiduous Japanese observer of T'ang life; Ennin's description of the great suppression of Buddhism in 842–45 is particularly valuable. Jacques Gernet gives a brilliant account of the role of Buddhism in Chinese economic life in *Les Aspects économiques du Bouddhisme dans la société chinoise du Ve au Xe siècle* (Saigon, 1956). L. S. Yang's article "Buddhist Monasteries and Four Money-Raising Institutions in Chinese History," *Harvard Journal of Asiatic Studies*, XIII (1950), is also important.

The noted Buddhist pilgrims of the T'ang left records which are of great importance for the study of Indian history and the history of Buddhism. Several of these have been translated, but the reader should be warned that most of the available translations are now out of date. Among these are Thomas

Watters, *On Yuan Chwang's [Hsüan-tsang's] Travels in India, 629–645* A.D. (London, 1904), and Junjiro Takakusu, *I Ching, A Record of the Buddhist Religion as Practised in India and the Malay Archipelago* (A.D. *671–695*) (Oxford, 1896). Arthur Waley has written a readable and accurate biography of Hsüan-tsang in *The Real Tripitaka* (London, 1952). A partial translation by Li Yung-hsi of the standard canonical account entitled *The life of Hsüan-tsang* appeared in Peking in 1959. Despite the devoted work of pilgrims and translators, the doctrinal cleavages between Chinese and Indian Buddhists were, by T'ang times, very great. A series of doctrinal discussions, between learned clerics of China and India, chaired by Tibetans, was held in the eighth century, and Paul Demiéville has analyzed the record of this debate in *Le Concile de Lhasa* (Paris, 1952).

For the period of the decline and appropriation of Buddhism, only a few studies exist in Western languages. One of these is Galen Eugene Sargent's analysis of the anti-Buddhist attitudes of the great formulator of neo-Confucianism Chu Hsi, published as *Tchou Hi contre le Bouddhisme* (Paris, 1955). Biographies of leading monks of the Sung dynasty (960–1279) are to be included in the large cyclopedia of Sung history and society which is being edited in Paris. Ferdinand Lessing's study of Lamaistic Buddhism as reflected in its principal Chinese temple, entitled *Yung Ho Kung, an Iconography of the Lamaist Cathedral in Peking* (Vol. I, Stockholm, 1942), gives valuable insights into a late form of Mahayana Buddhism favored particularly by non-Chinese dynasties.

For the recent history of Buddhism in China, a study based on close field observation is J. Prip-Møller, *Chinese Buddhist Monasteries* (Copenhagen, 1937). By far the most important works are three by Holmes Welch: *The Practice of Chinese*

Buddhism, 1900–1950 (Cambridge, Mass., 1967), which gives in fascinating detail the religious practices of the monastic communities, their organization and management; *The Buddhist Revival in China* (Cambridge, Mass., 1968), which deals with the whole effort to develop a "modernized" Buddhism for clergy and laity alike, with programs of publication, study groups, modern social service organs, etc.; *Buddhism Under Mao*, which will appear from the same press in 1972. It contains a detailed account of what has happened to the temples, the clerical communities, and the Buddhist laity since 1949. Revealing reminiscences of the Western convert who has spent the longest time in Chinese Buddhist monasteries are found in John Blofeld, *The Wheel of Life* (London, 1959).

TRANSLATIONS FROM CHINESE BUDDHIST TEXTS

Few anthologies of selections from Chinese Buddhist works exist. Perhaps the most useful is *Buddhist Texts Through the Ages* (New York, 1954), though the Chinese and Japanese texts translated by Arthur Waley occupy only the last thirty pages. *Sources of the Chinese Tradition*, edited by Wm. Theodore de Bary (New York, 1960) devotes pages 306–408 to translations of basic Chinese Buddhist texts; here they are placed in the context of Chinese intellectual and religious development. De Bary has also edited a convenient volume of translated excerpts entitled *The Buddhist Tradition in India, China and Japan* (New York, 1969).

The earliest surviving Chinese Buddhist apologetic, the *Li-huo lun*, was ably translated by Paul Pelliot as "Meou-tseu, ou les doutes levés," *T'oung-pao*, XIX (1920). One of the most important Chinese Buddhist texts of the period of disunion is the *Chao-lun* by Seng-chao, a leading disciple of the great translator Kumārajīva. This has been published in English translation by Walter Liebenthal as *The Book of Chao* (Peking, 1948). The Lotus sutra, one of the most influential of the Mahayana texts, was partially and imperfectly translated from the Chinese version by William E. Soothill as *The Lotus of the Wonderful Law* (Oxford, 1930). The *Vimalakīrti-nirdeśa*, which figured so largely in the Buddhism of the period of disunion and after, has been expertly translated by Etienne Lamotte as *L'Enseignement de Vimalakīrti* (Louvain, 1962). The appendix on Vimalakīrti in China by Paul Demiéville is of particular interest. One of the philosophical texts brought back and translated by Hsüan-tsang was Dharmapala's *Vijñaptimātratā-siddhi* ("Completion of Mere Ideation"). A complete translation by Louis de la Vallée Poussin was published as *La Siddhi de Hiuen-tsang* (2 vols., Paris, 1928–29; index volume, 1948). Another text, translated by Hsüan-tsang, became the basis for a philosophic sect of Sino-Japanese Buddhism. This was reconstructed and translated by de la Vallée Poussin as *L'Abhidharmakośa de Vasubandhu* (6 vols., Paris, 1923–31). Clarence Hamilton translated Hsüan-tsang's version of a much briefer statement of Vasubandhu's philosophy, *Wei Shih Er Shih Lun* (New Haven, 1938). We owe to Etienne Lamotte expert reconstructions and translations of two Mahayana texts which had an important influence on Chinese Buddhist philosophy. See *Le Traité de la grande vertu de sagesse de Nāgārjuna* (2 vols., Louvain, 1944–49) and *La Somme du Grand Véhicule d'Asanga (Mahāyāna-samgraha)* (3 vols., Louvain, 1944–70). Dr. Daisetz Suzuki's translation *The Lankavatara Sutra* (London, 1932) and a companion volume, *Studies in the Lankavatara Sutra* (London, 1930), interpret for the western reader a text which has long been esteemed and studied by the adherents of the Ch'an (Zen) school. A most influential text allegedly written by

Hui-neng, the founder of the Southern School of Zen, has been carefully analyzed and translated by Philip Yampolsky as *The Platform Sutra of the Sixth Patriarch* (New York, 1967).

A text with wide and continuing authority among Buddhists of many kinds is the *Ta Ch'eng ch'i-hsin lun*, attributed to Aśvaghośa. The pioneer translation is *Açvaghosha's Discourse on the Awakening of Faith in the Mahayana* by D. T. Suzuki (Chicago, 1900), superseded by Y. Hakeda, *The Awakening of Faith* (New York, 1967). Major Pure Land texts translated by Max Muller and J. Takakusu are included in *Sacred Books of the East*, Vol. XLIX (Oxford, 1894).

When one turns from expositions of doctrine to Buddhist literature, there is little that can be recommended with confidence. Edouard Chavannes' magnificent translations of the stories taken from the Indian Jātaka, or birth stories, and used to illustrate the workings of Buddhist principles may be read with pleasure and profit. See *Cinq cents contes et apologues* (3 vols., Paris, 1910–11). A recent collection by Richard Robinson, *Chinese Buddhist Verse* (London, 1954), gives the reader a glimpse of some varieties of hymns of praise, and of philosophical and moral poetry out of the vast corpus of such writings available in the Chinese Buddhist canon.

CHINESE BUDDHIST ART

There is no one work which surveys with authority this vast and complex field. The reader may use with confidence the recent work of Alexander Soper and Lawrence Sickman, *The Art and Architecture of China* (Baltimore, 1956), as a guide to the place of Buddhism in the total development of Chinese art. J. LeRoy Davidson has traced in a most revealing way the expression in Buddhist art of the ideas and motifs of a single influential sutra; see *The Lotus Sutra in Chinese Art* (New

Haven, 1954). The profusely illustrated volumes by Osvald Sirén, particularly his *Chinese Sculpture from the Fifth to the Fourteenth Century* (4 vols., London, 1925), give a good general view of the development of Chinese Buddhist art. See also his *Studies in Chinese Art and Some Indian Influences* (London, 1938). Unfortunately the great work of Tokiwa Daijō and Sekino Tadashi, *Shina Bukkyō shiseki* ("Chinese Buddhist Monuments") (5 cases of plates, 5 volumes of text, Tokyo, 1925–31), is now very scarce, and the five volumes of English text (Tokyo, 1926–38) are still harder to find.

The Tun-huang caves, whose discovery early in this century affected all fields of Chinese studies, contain a wealth of documentation on Chinese Buddhism from the fifth to the tenth century. Paul Pelliot's study of these caves is indispensable; see *Les Grottes de Touen-houang, peintures et sculptures bouddhiques des époques des Wei, des T'ang et des Song* (6 vols., Paris, 1914–24). A brief popular account, with some recent photographs, is Irene Vincent's *Sacred Oasis* (Chicago, 1953). The Peking government is now publishing in various forms reproductions of the wall paintings of Tun-huang, but so far these have been limited to prints of artists' copies of the pictures.

The most complete account of a major Buddhist monument is Seiichi Mizuno and Toshio Nagahiro, *Yün-Kang, The Buddhist Cave-Temples of the Fifth Century A.D. in North China* (16 volumes, Kyoto, 1951–56; other volumes to come). The plates are of incomparable clarity, and though the full text is in Japanese, there are helpful English captions and summaries.

To get an impression of current studies of Chinese Buddhist art by Western scholars, the reader may look into recent issues of such journals as *Artibus Asiae, The Art Bulletin, Ars Orientalis,* and the *Archives of the Chinese Art Society of America.*

INDEX